SHAKING HANDS WITH WISDOM

Dr. Ron Webb

Copyright © 2020 by **Dr. Ron Webb**

All rights reserved. No part of this publication may be reproduced by any means, graphics, electronic, or mechanical, including photocopying, recording, taping, or by any information storage retrieval system without the written permission of the publisher except in the case of brief quotations embodied in critical articles and reviews.

**Dr. Ron Webb/Rejoice Essential Publishing
PO BOX 512
Effingham, SC 29541**

www.republishing.org

Unless otherwise indicated, scripture is taken from the King James Version.

Scripture quotations marked (NIV) are taken from the Holy Bible, New International Version®, NIV®. Copyright © 1973, 1978, 1984, 2011 by Biblica, Inc.™ Used by permission of Zondervan. All rights reserved worldwide. www.zondervan.com The "NIV" and "New International Version" are trademarks registered in the United States Patent and Trademark Office by Biblica, Inc.™

Shaking Hands with Wisdom/ Dr. Ron Webb

ISBN-13: 978-1-952312-04-5

Library of Congress Control Number: 2020904023

In honor of Arlie Sandusky and the legacy he will leave behind!

"We learn from leaning on legends." — Dr. Ron Webb

ACKNOWLEDGEMENTS

I want to first and foremost, thank my family for their love and support. I am forever grateful to the fathers who have served as mentors in my life and throughout my years of ministry. I would like to thank my father, the late Alfonse Webb, Sr., and my spiritual fathers in the ministry the late Bishop James Price, Bishop Charles Rodgers, Dr. Larry Simmons, and Jim Bakker. I am also thankful to my other mentors: the late Clinton Summers, the late Jasper Edmondson, Benny Robertson, Harry Blackwell, Dr. John Hagler, and Coach Gene Bess.

Dr. Ron Webb

***

I give honor to God for all He has done in my life and for using us as a vessel to distribute revelation and knowledge regarding the importance of mentorship. I honor my pastor and mentor, whom I have been given the opportunity to share a vision with, and through hard work and dedication, see it come to pass. God knew that the world needed a book on the firsthand experience about mentorship and what better way than to have the mentor and the mentee join together and share stories, examples, and warnings when it comes to mentorship and the importance of partnership. The world needs a better you, and to lead effectively, you must follow humbly. It is a privilege to serve and to pour into others as God pours into you. I pray that this book encourages you to live for something greater and to follow the guidance and leadership needed to become all that God created you to be. Godspeed in all your endeavors, and always listen to the voice of wisdom.

Amber M. Brown
Evangelist/Author of Rise To The Mission, Co-Author Shaking Hands with Wisdom

TABLE OF CONTENTS

ACKNOWLEDGMENTS vii

PREFACE xii

INTRODUCTION 1

CHAPTER 1:   Shaking Hands with Wisdom 4

CHAPTER 2:   Passing the Baton 9

CHAPTER 3:   Wax On Wax Off 15

CHAPTER 4:   Spirit of an Orphan 18

CHAPTER 5:   Undeveloped Leaders 22

CHAPTER 6:   Winning Moments of Wisdom 25

CHAPTER 7:   A Soldier in Two Armies 32

CHAPTER 8:   Someone Paved the Way 41

CHAPTER 9:   Cultivating the Legacy 44

CHAPTER 10:   The Role of a Mentee 48

CHAPTER 11:   Mentorship Provides a Covering 53

CHAPTER 12:	Fathers of the Faith	57
CHAPTER 13:	The Greatest Mentor of Them All	61
CHAPTER 14:	The Jethro Principle	65
CHAPTER 15:	Mentorship Through a Book	69
CHAPTER 16:	Out of Order	73
CHAPTER 17:	Don't Underestimate Distractions	78
CHAPTER 18:	Mentoring Moments	82
CHAPTER 19:	Open Book	88
CHAPTER 20:	Take a Chance on Me	92
CHAPTER 21:	Join Me at the Table	95
CHAPTER 22:	Can You Trust the Process?	99
CHAPTER 23:	Right Place Right Time	103
ABOUT THE AUTHORS		106

PREFACE

IRON SHARPENS IRON

Proverbs 27:17 says, "Iron sharpens iron." We can all grow and learn from one another along this journey, especially in a mentor-mentee relationship. I must admit, I highly respect the wisdom of days and years, while we're in a generation that admires strength physically, there's another strength we experience through wisdom and the mentoring of others. Yes, Jesus said, "I called you young men because you're strong and overcome the wicked one. I call the old men to counsel for your wisdom." While this book is written to encourage every mentee to find a mentor, because mentors help navigate through difficult situations. It's also an opportunity for juniors to draw from the wells of seniors. Mentees need a mentor to take them to the next level in whatever area they are being mentored. Mentees must be humble and realize that there is still room for them to grow while serving the mentor's vision so they can be sharpened in the process.

As mentors are pouring themselves into their mentees, they are being sharpened as well. Why? Because the mentee is drawing from the well of wisdom inside, and this is a great opportunity to train, equip, and impart. Mentors can't be selfish or intimidated by those they are called to lead. They must realize that they are vicariously reaching everyone their mentee potentially will impact. Seniors have something to give because we all have stood on the shoulders of giants. I'm so thankful for mentors because they see things in you that you don't see in yourself. We should always cherish the wisdom of the fathers of faith. God put them here for our benefit. Their wisdom is priceless; let's take advantage of every opportunity afforded to us. I was so blessed by my elder's experiences-the stories they told, all of what I heard blessed my soul, and I pray that one day I'm able to pass on the wisdom that I received.

INTRODUCTION

Mentoring and coaching are similar, but not the same terms. They often get used interchangeably, which can mislead the audience. Both are similar in the development of someone, but each involves very different disciplines in practices.

Mentoring consists of long-term relationships focusing on the support and development of the mentee or protégé. The mentor becomes a source of wisdom, teaching, and support, but not always monitoring specific behavior or actions of others. Coaching typically involves a relationship of finite duration with a focus on strengthening or eliminating specific behaviors in the here and now.

The mentee's responsibility is to identify the mentor and establish a relationship. Let's discuss and compare expectations for both the mentors and the mentees.

1. Although the mentor doesn't appear in the Bible, the Scriptures give many examples of it. Eli mentored Samuel. Elijah mentored Elisha. Barnabas mentored Paul. Naomi mentored Ruth. Jesus mentored the disciples. Jesus said, "Come let me make you fishers of men." The word "mentor" means to advise or a trusted counselor or teacher. Jethro mentored Moses and through wise counsel, he spoke wisdom to Moses and protected him from burning out. Yes! Moses was wearing away, but he provided a plan to sustain him and also sustain the people. Every Moses needs a Jethro to speak into their lives.

2. Moses mentored Joshua. God told Moses to put some of his glory upon him. Test them before you tag them. Allow them to make mistakes and show them how to correct them. Then after Moses died, Joshua stepped up to the plate and led the charge. Joshua was able to take the people to another level, then he mentors the other remaining leaders of the army. But the sad thing is after Joshua and the elders died, then arose another generation that didn't have mentors. Everybody did what was right in their own eyes. No guidance, they did what they wanted to do. See the danger of not having mentors?

Discipleship and mentorship are vital for the next generation because it results in us being changed agents. We walk alongside the mentees by showing them how to love and serve God. God provided mentors in the family also family mentorship. We must pass down wisdom from generation to generation.

"Hear O Israel: The Lord our God, the Lord is one. Love the Lord your God with all your heart and with all your soul and with all your strength. These commandments that I give you today are to be upon your hearts. Impress them on your children. Talk about them when you sit at home and when you walk along the road, when you lie down and when you get up. Tie them as symbols on your hands and bind them on your foreheads. Write them on the doorframes of your houses and on your gates." — Deuteronomy 6:4-9 (NIV)

"Shake the hand that feeds you."

— Michael Pollan

CHAPTER 1

SHAKING HANDS WITH WISDOM

Shaking Hands with Wisdom was birthed out of a general conversation, and many interviews with the generals who God has graced to stay here. They continue to show us the road map to success by giving us wisdom on how to avoid the pits and potholes that cause failure. Thank you for sharing your personal experiences of the good, the bad, and the ugly. Yes, we need wisdom of the old, in conjunction with the strength of the youth. They both work together hand in hand. The Bible has much to say about wisdom. Proverbs 9:10 says, "The fear of the Lord is the beginning of wisdom."

Wisdom is the principal thing, but in all your getting, get an understanding (Proverbs 4:7). Solomon asked God for wisdom (2 Chronicles 1:7-10).

There are bountiful benefits that come with the wisdom package, knowing what won't work is just as important as knowing what will work. Knowing what not to do as much as knowing what to do comes through wisdom. Wisdom provides protection, direction, and correction.

Now, I understand that we have an age where almost everything is only a fingertip away. In some ways, it is good, but with all the answers at our fingertips, the information cannot answer most of the questions that matter the most. Even though we're swimming in 24/7 news, media personalities, and opinions, it is overwhelming to the point that we wonder what's really legit. Is it true or not true?! Statistics say that we're the most anxious plagued, depressed ridden culture in the history of the world. Think about this, we are the most educated and informed generation, more than any culture in the history of the world, but still something is missing. It's something Google can't answer, and it is something the universities can't teach. My friends, that something is the wisdom of God.

Wisdom is just simply using knowledge the right way. Wisdom knows how to speak but also knows when to speak. Wisdom not only knows what to say but how to say it. Some things can't be taught; it must be caught! Yes, I understand it is the information, but at the same time seeking knowledge is one thing, but obtaining wisdom is another. We need the wisdom of God in our business dealings because of corruption and dishonesty. When we pray for the wisdom of God and seek Him by acknowledging Him in all of our ways, He will direct our path.

We need the wisdom of God in our marriage!

So many couples are divorcing and can't agree on anything. We need the wisdom of God on how to handle and interact with our spouses. The wisdom of God teaches us how and when to pursue a matter. It also teaches us when to shut our mouths and go pray about it. The wisdom of God in marriages will help men to become better husbands as they learn how to lead their families. Women will become better wives as they submit to their husbands while he takes the leadership role.

We need the wisdom of God to raise our children!

It is such a challenge now, but through the wisdom of God, we learn how to approach our children with kindness and not provoke them and overly correct them. What we do right now in our children's lives will impact them forever. We must make sure that we are instilling godly attributes in them, so when they get older, they will not depart from what they were taught. When our children reach adulthood, they will be a representation of us. God's wisdom will ensure that they succeed.

We need the wisdom of God to lead God's people!

We must know how to lead God's people in a world with so many negative influences. People have different personalities, backgrounds, and viewpoints, and having the wisdom of God is essential. Some people may get easily offended or operate in the wrong spirit. God will show us how to handle these difficult situations as we seek Him.

When people want to serve or volunteer in our ministries or businesses, we need to pray to place the right people in the right job or position. If the wrong person is out of place, then the ministry or business won't flow smoothly. The wrong person in place could be someone who has the wrong motives concerning you and the vision of the Lord concerning the ministry or business. Also, they might not be the most qualified for the job and can do more damage than good.

Next, when wisdom is in operation, we learn how to set healthy boundaries between a mentor-mentee relationship. If not, then the mentee can mistake their mentor as a friend and won't heed to their correction or guidance. Some people may want to connect to you because of your name, a platform, and who you know. When they get what they want from you, then they will discard and sever the relationship. Others may want to spend hours every day on the phone, and when you aren't able, they might get offended and find another mentor. Most likely, a mentor might be too busy and will have to prioritize their time. Establishing boundaries at the beginning of every relationship is the key to a long lasting one.

Lastly, having God's wisdom will allow us to be a great example as we are duplicating ourselves in the lives of our mentees. We are depositing a portion of our spirits just as Elijah did with Elisha. People can see who has trained and poured into a person when they began to take on specific characteristics of their mentor. They may sound like their leaders as they preach or do other activities.

We must pray for spiritual direction, as Solomon prayed for God's wisdom. We must also ask God to give us the wisdom to lead His people and to settle conflict because we're going to have disagreements and, in most cases, people lean to the flesh, and they try to settle the score on their own.

"The greatest act of leadership is mentoring. No matter how much you may learn, achieve, accumulate, or accomplish, if it all dies with you, then you are a generational failure."

Myles Munroe

CHAPTER 2

PASSING THE BATON

There is nothing more valuable than a covering, and the greatest part of mentorship is knowing that it never ends. While in the process, it is expected to pass on the wisdom and experience gained to the next person, but many do not understand the need for it. Most people today are more worried about power and position for themselves. Still, our goal for humanity is not self-gain, but rather forming relationships from the older generation to the younger in hopes that the world will go on and prosper! Many of us have taken roads that were not meant for travel that led us to dead ends. Some paths have turned out to be a blessing, but wrong turns were still made. Then other roads haven't even had the chance to be traveled. Why? Because no one has led you there.

It is much easier to lead someone down the road of success when you have already traveled it. The road less traveled tends to be the roughest because not many have had to conquer it. But the greatness of those who have made it to the end, lies in the fact that they live to tell it. There is an unmet need to lay the foundation and build the bridge that will be the transition for the next generation. Four problems are arising in this age:
1. Self-serving attitudes of the young
2. Non-committed presence of the old

3. Intimidation experienced by the older generation
4. A wounded older generation

The younger generation has lost the principle of serving others instead of themselves. Philippians 2:3 says, "Do nothing from selfish ambition or conceit, but in humility count others more significant than yourselves." They must have the right motives and count their mentor's vision, business, or ministry more highly than their own. God is pleased when our hearts are pure in His sight.

Some may feel like their ministry won't go forward while they are serving underneath someone's leadership. They may think, "God, what about my ministry?" Your assignment will prosper, and you will have everything that you need because you will reap what you have sown. Luke 16:12 (NIV) says, "And if you have not been trustworthy with someone else's property, who will give you property of your own?" As the younger generation is serving, God will make sure the right doors open for them. Whatever you make happen for others, God will make sure it will happen for you.

The older generation must make themselves available to the younger generation — the old need to be committed and be there in the lives of the youth. When you first came into something new, you probably had so many questions and wished someone was available to help. The younger generation feels the same. They need the wisdom that you carry. Make time for them so they won't make the same mistakes. It's hard work, but the reward is great.

The older generation can't be intimidated by the anointing, talents, and gifts of the younger generation. Just because you are older doesn't make you insignificant or obsolete. You are valuable, so there's no need to compete and suppress others because of insecurity. Your ministry or business won't die, but it will get better as you pour into others. The older generation doesn't need to be a Saul trying to kill the uprising Davids. The fruitfulness of your mentorship will show through your mentees when they are doing greater exploits.

Sometimes the older generation may carry wounds because their mentees have hurt them. They genuinely love people, but the wrong person mistreated them, resulting in them putting up a wall. Once this shield is up, then they are resistant to the idea of mentorship. They may have made inner vows and said, "I will never train or disciples ever again," which are the wrong thoughts to have. Not everyone is a snake, opportunist, Jezebel, Absalom, or demonized. Some people are called to sit underneath your leadership because they need the oil that's on your life. Get before the Lord so you can be made whole. When wholeness occurs, you will get past the hurt and disappointment and be ready to pour into a willing vessel.

Without the presence of the wise, another soul lies dormant. Thus, when you kill one, you kill them all! When you give up on pushing one person forward, you give up on every single one after them.

As the late Dr. Myles Munroe said before his passing, "We must start passing the baton." What we must understand in this generation is that the wisdom of the old must be passed down to the young or else it will die with you, and then where does that leave those that are still here? What happens to the school systems, churches, government, or agriculture? It can't all stop with you. The ways to a better life, the wisdom of leadership, and the skills of success cannot be buried with you! The world must keep going forward and we want it to be even greater for the next generation!

Myles Munroe was one of the greatest leaders and evangelists of his time. Dr. Munroe, his wife, and seven others passed away in a plane crash while traveling to a leadership conference in 2014. Before the crash, he spoke about a dream he had and the meaning behind it. Dr. Munroe spoke prophetically about leaders preparing to pass the baton to the next generation. We must step up and be willing to learn as the younger generation, but also the older generation must learn how to step down and pull the next one up to help pave the way for success of the future generations.

In Munroe's dream, a track and field athlete was lying in his coffin, clutching a baton. Munroe said that the dream was about people dying with a baton instead of passing it on. He said, "I was thinking, the young person who's supposed to lead next has to go to the casket, pry the baton out of the dead man's hand just to take it to the next leg." Then he said, "Great leaders pass [the baton] on before they die, and they live to see the other person run."

Wow! What a dream. Just take a moment to picture that in your mind. Picture yourself running, and it's time to grab the baton from the next runner's hand, but you can't. You are pulling and pulling, but they won't let it go. Now, you've slowed down and the next person ahead of you is delayed because they are relying on you to get there before they can go, and until you get there, they must wait. No one likes looking down at their watch waiting when they have a scheduled appointment to get to, and the same applies in this situation.

Munroe's son, Myles Chairo Munroe, was interviewed after his father passed. He said, "We will not allow death to claim any victory, but we celebrate the life and legacy of each individual. This tragedy does not mark the end; the end of life, the end of a vision, the end of a journey, nor the end of a purpose, but it marks the new beginning of a new era." Then he said, "A 'new generation' will carry on the vision and legacy that his parents built." Then he quoted one of his father's quotes: "The greatest tragedy in life is not death but is in dying without a purpose." Chairo said, "We know there is a greater purpose in all of this.

We are now the vessels for this new vision and this new legacy to be carried on."

You are a valuable piece in carrying on the legacy. If you don't, who will? You can't wait on others to do it, because each one of us is called to take care of one another and to take care of this world. It is our responsibility to serve and to teach; to follow and to lead! You can choose to be like others and die with the baton in your hand, but I say think about your children, grandchildren, nieces, nephews, friends, and family. You want them all to live a better life and not to make the same mistakes you made, right? Well, now is the time to rise and start preparing to pass the baton. There is power in mentorship and that power comes from within you. Don't be a generational failure. Don't die with the baton in your hand, but pass it on and be the one who lives to watch others carry it on!

"Wax on, right hand. Wax off, left hand. Wax on, wax off."

— Mr. Miyagi

CHAPTER 3

"WAX ON WAX OFF"

Most of us remember the movie the Karate Kid. Mr. Miyagi becomes Daniel's teacher and slowly becomes a surrogate father figure to him. He begins Daniel's training by having him perform laborious chores such as waxing a car, sanding a wooden floor, refurbishing a fence, and painting his house. Each chore is accomplished with a mission and a specific movement such as counterclockwise and clockwise hand motion.

Now, the interesting thing is Daniel sees no connection to his training coming from these chores. Eventually, he becomes frustrated, believing he has learned nothing of karate. Still, when he began to vent his frustration, Mr. Miyagi reveals to Daniel that he has been learning defensive blocks through muscle memory through performing chores.

Then later his trainer shows him all the tasks he has been doing and that they are transferable to karate. Still, it's only at the end when Daniel realizes all that seems to be crazy and doesn't make sense can pay off in the long run. "Wax on, wax off" was one of the stern instructions repeated at the beginning of each lesson.

When your mentor wants you to complete an assignment, you might not see the point, but there is a reason. Remember these words from Karate Kid, "Wax on, wax off." You may think that you are ready to preach, teach, or step out, but your mentor may feel otherwise because they can see the immaturity and the further need for character development. Instead of agreeing with you, they may tell you to clean up the church, work the book table, tarry with others at the altar, hold the camera, pass out flyers, etc. These acts of service require walking in love and humility. In obedience to leadership, much fruit will be developed over time. You will be well prepared for challenges that may arise and qualified for your assignment.

I believe it's important to note that you must trust your trainer or mentor. They see potential in you, gifts, and talents that you don't see in yourself. They also can bring it out of you. There are some skills that you can learn on your own, but if you intend to take the journey of mastery, the best thing you can do is connect with first rate instruction. For mastering most skills, the best things you can do is end up in the hands of a master teacher, and trust me that will serve as your payoff.

"The hallmark of an orphan spirit is the survivor mentality. The mentality that says, 'I am not loved and relationships do not last.' This is the very spirit that God sent His Son to deliver us from."

— Kylo

CHAPTER 4

SPIRIT OF AN ORPHAN

First and foremost, one of the greatest needs in the Body of Christ is the need for spiritual fathers. Apostle Paul wrote in 1 Corinthians 4:15 that we have few fathers, but have many instructors and many teachers. After reading that Scripture, I was led to write about the orphan spirit. Even though they have been born again and adopted in the family of God as sons, they still feel hindered in moving forward in the things of God.

Let's take a moment and describe this spirit of an orphan. Deep down, people struggle within to be accepted, the need to be loved, affirmed, and noticed. They are very insecure and very unsure of their place in the family. I need to write about this because I have found my desire to reach out and try to help mentor sons and daughters in the ministry. Some are reluctant or have a spirit of withdrawal. It is hard for them to trust. Why? Because many have dealt with the spirit of abandonment, and unhealed hurts from their past. So, don't feel as a mentor that you're not doing your part, it really has nothing to do with you, it's their own feelings of insecurity.

I must confess I somewhat took it personally when reaching out to a young man trying to help him, but he would not reach back. He had such an independent spirit, but he was always seeking affirmation. Always wanting to be complimented, always asking, "Is this okay or do you like this?" It was like he wanted a grade for his performance, not realizing that God loves us for who we are, not what we do.

Once there was an individual who wanted to connect with me because they thought I could launch their ministry. They saw everything that God was doing in my life and wanted the same. They said, "I'm with you for the long haul, and I am submitting myself underneath you to learn." These words sounded sweet, but over time the truth was revealed about their character and the orphan spirit inside. This person jumped from ministry to ministry, and as I did my research, they had a long track record of doing so. They broke covenant relationships and ended up feeling confused at times because of the conflicting information they heard various preachers say. I told this person that they can't eat from everyone's table and gently reproved them. This individual tried to cause division in my ministry, and after another rebuke, they left. Their pride caused them not to receive me as a mentor anymore but now they are my equal. Since the disconnection, I have watched them connect with several other ministries. The orphan spirit will make a person feel like everyone is against them, and they don't belong. This spirit needs to be cast out and confronted so the mentee won't end relationships prematurely instead of being delivered from the offense.

So, I want to set someone free today from feeling like you must perform or the feeling of being rejected, alienated, or lonely. So, while trying to mentor someone with an orphan spirit can be at the least a challenge, it prepares one for a long path to freedom, and remember don't get offended. Just realize that many have dealt with these feelings long before you showed up and because of this spirit, it has caused a disconnect in marriages, ministries, businesses, and many other areas of their lives. So, your assignment of mentoring may not be to show them how to build a house, how to speak before large crowds, or perfect their gifts. Maybe in this season, your assignment is to show or express the Father's love and His affirmation.

"When you run a part of the relay and pass on the baton, there is no sense of unfinished business in your mind. There is just the sense of having done your part to the best of your ability. That is it. The hope is to pass on the baton to somebody who will run faster and run a better marathon."

— N. R. Narayana Murthy

CHAPTER 5

UNDEVELOPED LEADERS

It has been repeatedly said that good followers make good leaders. It's tough to lead if you have never been led, which is why we end up with leaders who are not developed. Someone who is undeveloped is lacking growth and sometimes lacking confidence and the tools you need to grow: loyalty, commitment, dedication, and steadfastness. The question is, "Why do you lack development?"

Let's consider a seed that you plant in poor soil that has barely enough water and very little sunshine. How do you think that seed would grow? Not very well at all. But on the other hand, you plant the seed in good soil with plenty of sunshine and lots of water. That same seed would grow, flourish, and experience constant growth. The seed must be introduced to the right environment. There are some undeveloped leaders because they are simply in the wrong environment.

There is a danger of promoting unprepared leaders. It's like putting a kid behind a steering wheel of a car or a tractor, giving them the keys to drive or letting kids play with knives. It is an accident waiting to happen. My brother Terry joined the Boys Scouts at an early age in life. I can remember him earning his to-tin' chip award. To earn it, you must learn and demonstrate that you know how to carry and sharpen a knife, ax, and saw. It is a safety program to prevent injury to yourself and others while camping. They teach you how to collect firewood and to build campfires, but just think for a moment. Tools like knives, axes, saws are only dangerous when used inappropriately. But if you put them in the hands of untrained, unskilled people, it could be very dangerous.

There once was a prophet who had an international ministry. He started preaching as a small boy; however, he didn't have many mentors. As his ministry grew, pride, lust, deception, greed, and perversion set in his heart. Those around him tried to tell him about his ways, but he cut off the relationships. People were drawn to him because his gifts were extremely accurate, yet his character was terrible. Consecutive scandals came to light, and eventually, the truth was exposed. After everything came out, the prophet continued to sin, and many people were affected by it. Some people backslid, and others put their guard up concerning prophets. Character development is a must, so people aren't hurt, and our Lord Jesus isn't put to shame. There is value in having people around us that will tell us, "No. That's not right. That's wrong." These voices will help us stay on the straight and narrow path if we take heed.

So, it is when we place untrained, untested, undeveloped, unskilled people in leadership and give inexperienced leaders tools they don't know how to use, it becomes detrimental to them and others. My simple advice is to please seek out training and mentorship from experienced leaders. There is a danger in appointing untrained, undeveloped leaders. You, as a mentor, have to evaluate their readiness. Never guess at it. Evaluate skill levels and be honest in your evaluation. Tell them where they're lacking so that they can learn from you. Remember, a dull ax requires lots of work. It's okay to say, "I need more help then what I'm getting."

"There is a destiny which makes us brothers; none goes his way alone. All that we send into the lives of others comes back into our own."

— Edwin Markham

CHAPTER 6

WINNING MOMENTS OF WISDOM

In interviewing "The Most Winningest Coach in America," Coach Gene Bess said, "My greatest joy as a coach and mentor is in knowing how my players do after they leave." Coaches are great mentors, and if you are a great one, then you make an effort to follow up with your players and visit them even after they leave to ensure they are applying what they've learned. It is your responsibility to be a mentor and a coach even after the ball is bouncing!

For someone who has been coaching for 50+ years, he has extensive experience in training the young and has learned that mentorship holds great value, especially if it is from someone who has been there. From a coaching standpoint, it is important to follow up with your player, just like it is essential to follow up with your mentee. Many people fall short and do not follow up with those they have previously poured into because they find themselves needing to pour into the uprising mentees. Yet, taking the time to do this as a coach and as a mentor is vital.

I want to thank Coach Bess for mentoring me on and off the court. Also, I want to thank him for being a strong leader and teaching me to never give up, never give in, and to never stop.

I am forever grateful and appreciative of his leadership. I want to thank Coach Bess for giving me the opportunity to preach my first sermon. He saw the gifts and talents in my life. He believed in me, which empowered me to go forth and fulfill my God-given assignment. I still remember the experience like it was yesterday, we were all at the hotel. Coach Bess called all the basketball players into the room and I gave a ten-minute sermon. I am grateful that Coach Bess was one of the first Christian role models that made a significant impact on my life. For that reason, I thank him and have stayed connected to him throughout the years.

Coaching a player forces a special relationship, which is hard to find in any other area of life. It's almost like a father figure to some. You always hear that kids are changing, and "this generation is not how we were," but really parents have changed more than kids. It is because of this that the youth are not like the youth from past generations. Young people still want the same thing. They want to be successful and they want someone who will get them to accomplish to the greatest degree possible!

A mentor should feel a special unction towards wanting to help each mentee just as a coach feels a special unction to help each player be the best. One of the things that I remembered, as a player, is resenting when coaches didn't challenge players. Those that took the easy way out and did not get in a hectic situation just to avoid conflict. As a coach and a mentor, you have to face up to all kinds of circumstances where you are helping players and mentees get better and sometimes that involves dialogue. Not just on the court but off the court. A coach and a mentor can be so many things in the lives of his or her players. But the question is, "Who are you with your players? Who do you choose to be with your mentee?"

A coach needs to be themselves, so in mentorship, you must also be yourself. Everyone is unique and for the most part, a mentor wants to be as politically correct as they can be, and yet they must remain themselves. In coaching, you must be consistent as with mentoring in whatever area that you mentor, you must remain consistent. It is not until you know who you are that you can effectively help someone. When they see a mentor changing gears and going back and forth, it's easy to assume that they can do the same, which makes it hard to teach consistency.

There are many years ahead and so many things to learn, whether you are the mentor or the mentee. The coach or the player. The teacher or the student. You cannot do this on your own. Without God placing people in your life to help lead you in the direction He wants you to go, it'll be hard to make it to your final destination. The younger generation should want to be teachable, want to learn, and not want to do it on our own, but we find many without guidance and direction. The reason you continue to win is that you continue to learn! Fixing mistakes and learning from them or having a mentor that will teach you not to make the mistake they did is the best lesson of all. When you listen to wisdom, wisdom will speak!

Mentees have so many vices they can get into that keeps them from doing what they want or need to do to be successful: from drugs to social media, especially in the younger generation. You must reach people but not be sucked into the norm. You must grow, but not be confused about where you are going.

In looking for a mentee or mentor, there is a commonality between coach and player. A coach is trying to develop a player to have a degree of success and the player is trying to improve themselves so that they can play at a higher level. The same goes for mentorship with anything else. A mentor develops the mentee for success while the mentee improves their gifts to operate at a higher level.

Many mentees are talented and gifted but unreliable and not realizing how vital their general behavior, attitude, and actions.

For example, kids these days grow up and are allowed to misbehave at home knowing that if they throw a tantrum, they will get their way. So, when you inherit them as a mentor, you must now teach them that the behavior that they are used to will no longer be tolerated. It is hard for the young to look up to the old and be obedient when trust issues and home problems are present. There comes a time when you have to say that, "I want more." Most of the time, it's not because they aren't capable; it is because they aren't motivated.

As a coach, you must teach players to continue pushing regardless if they make it pro or not just as a mentor in any other area should push a mentee regardless if failure comes once or twice. The biggest thing we see in sports is that players don't realize how important academics are. The interest only in sports is not the real world, just like the interest in success only for the mentee is not the real world. You must be able to hold yourself at the level that you want to go at some point — not always relying on your mentor for everything. In basketball, if the players don't pass their classes, they won't even be able to play on the court. Well, if the mentee does not grow individually, then they will not be able to continue growing at the level that the mentor is leading them.

Some mentors even find themselves going through the most emotional things and difficult things, and it is not until then that they find a greater purpose. For example, when you lose a child, you think about how God sent His only begotten son to die for us being the greatest loss any human being can have is their child. Coach Bess said that he realized after losing his son that nothing in life could be more difficult, but he knew what he had to do now. He had to coach and develop the young! He said, "My son's death caused growth in me! It pushed me to want to be the best mentor I could be to other children."

The way you handle others as a mentor will determine your success. We all have a position to play. What we experienced in life plays a significant part in your mentoring than you even realize. We are what we put into others to develop them. Coach Gene Bess gave us some advice to consider:

1. When someone's wrong in a situation, do you correct them or stay silent?
If you don't speak up, it's the same thing as you agreeing with them. Many don't speak up, they allow others to, but as a mentor, you must call their hand on it. Many have wanted to play on a team but not be coached, so in turn, the coaches respected their wishes. As a result, they never got the teaching and wisdom in helping with the fundamentals.

2. How does pride affect someone from being mentored?
It keeps them from achieving goals only to come to a place when they realize that they are not where they should be. Lacking in fundamentals does become present. You want to be at a higher level, but you're not there because you didn't get the little lessons. The mentoring that you feel wasn't necessary was needed to achieve what you want gradually.

3. How can determination help you to succeed in mentorship?
Mentorship on the court is the same kind of mentorship on the field and in the classroom. It all needs the same attention and the same determination to succeed!

4. Do you agree that mentorship consists of different levels?
Yes, mentorship consists of many levels. A lot of people see themselves at a certain level, but really in all reality are not there yet. It takes a mentor to show them that just as it takes a coach to show a player that they need more teaching, and more fundamentals of the game before being thrown into the game! You

must look and see the needs of the player. You might not always have the same type of person to mentor, so every level is a challenge. But remember the better job the coach does at coaching the players, the more likely the team is to be better next year. That is the same as leading as a mentor.

"Every day in some way you are a part of a team. The question is not, will you participate in something that involves others? The question is, will your involvement with others be successful?"

— John C Maxwell

CHAPTER 7

A SOLDIER IN TWO ARMIES

Showing up is 90% of the battle! Everyone is given the same opportunity to show up, but here's the thing, not everyone will! The art of proficiency is not given, but it is earned. As a child, you don't start out walking, but you learn how to work your way into taking that first step. That is when strength and wisdom will take you to that next stage of life, shaping you and molding you for your future. You may fall a couple of times before learning the gradual motion of putting one foot in front of the other, but after much effort and direction, you eventually stand up on your own, you look at your target, and GO!

We were built to learn, then do, and then teach, but many find themselves turned in the opposite direction with no one helping to lead the way, and that is where accountability comes into play. Not only does God have a high regard for accountability when it comes to His children, but the training in which a soldier shows up not only builds success but creates a successful accountable individual.

The problem in today's society is that those that have been through the process of learning are not allowing themselves time to serve in the area in which they have been taught. They go directly into trying to teach other people how to do something they have never truly done themselves. How can you portray yourself to be a soldier when you haven't even gone through basic training? It is one thing to see others doing something, but until you learn by doing it on your own, how can you effectively teach another person and lead them in the direction of success? I could tell you how to shoot a gun or how to save a life, but if I've never done it myself or went through the training for it, then how could you really hold me accountable to give you what you needed? In general, this leaves millennials hungry for wisdom and direction, but they look around and see no one insight, which is why most are now joining the military. Not everyone truly wants to join at first but learn to appreciate it. Some are forcing themselves due to a lack of mentorship outside of the military. People truly want direction! Why do they join you ask? Because they are hungry for structure, answers, and for a win! When there is no accountability, success is not an option. We see many ready to learn but have no idea where to start. A new generation is being birthed. Without positive reinforcement, direction, and discipline, it is going to be that much harder to keep this world afloat without sinking.

Mutual Respect

One of the most important qualities of a soldier is that before he gets put into battle, he learns respect! A mentor and a mentee must be willing to give mutual respect just as on the battlefield with a sergeant and the soldier in training. The mentor and mentee in the marketplace are soldiers in this game called "life" and life must go on. We all need a Paul, a Barnabas, and a Timothy. You see, Paul pulls into your life and adds to what you have while teaching you how to subtract some things that are just holding you down. Barnabas is there as your "Spirit of Encouragement" and we all know that encouragement goes a long way. Timothy pushes you into your future and tells you to never give up! Do you recall having one of these types of mentors in your life?

Good things and good people bring discipline and correction to our lives. These are some important things to remember in the Army of Mentorship:

- You may or may not be a soldier in the military, but we are all soldiers in the Army of Mentorship!
- You need words of wisdom as a mentee just as a soldier needs his orders.
- Never forget that what you say matters. What you say, you must do as mentors, but also as mentees.
- As a mentor, you must pass on the mantle to those whom you speak into their lives. Just as a soldier takes on the uniform, the mentee also takes on the mantle.
- You must be willing to lead and follow. A good leader is always led by another while also mentoring someone else.
- A mentor must carry an anointing that is moving and not stagnant just as a sergeant must always be prepared to move as the soldier must always be ready to proceed with his trainer.
- People learn in different ways. Some are visual, while others do better on an intellectual level. Always remember to teach others and instruct them to make it easier for them to learn so that you don't have to keep repeating the same things. Pay attention to those "teachable moments".
- It's okay to make mistakes, but make sure you don't keep making the same ones. Just as a teacher addresses problems in a classroom, the focus is on bettering the students and allowing them to see what it could be like without the same mistakes, not just to make rules that will not have a lasting benefit on the student.

Establish Training Methods

As a mentor, you must establish a relationship and teach authoritatively no matter who you are mentoring. A sergeant is always the same way with every soldier and teaches the same way with them. But a teacher and a student, for example, the training method is a different scenario. A very wise pastor told me, "Sometimes as teachers you find yourself so far removed from a student's needs making policies and rules for the day, but if you don't understand who you're working with, that policy or rule can very well be out of date," and this is so true. Not only do we teach soldiers in the military how to effectively become men of great stature on and off the battlefield, but we also teach our children that we all can have the same opportunities. Also, we all play a role in this world and out of the classroom.

A Story Behind Every Action

There is always a story behind an action! Mentorship can be rough, and mistakes can be made just like a soldier on the battlefield or a student in the classroom. But our job is to not just find out the story as a mentor but also learn about the journey as a mentee.

- Mentors, as you know the story of your mentee, you will then understand how to teach them and what they need to be successful.
- It is so important that you are passionate about what you do. A mentor needs to show cause! Be able to relate and don't be afraid to let your mentee know that you have been through the very same things yourself. Relevance is key!

It is interesting that when you're in the military, they strip you of your identity. They mold you into a team mentality, but the very time that a mentor addresses a problem with a mentee, they get offended and want to quit. There are many reasons why this can happen, but the most obvious reason pertaining to mentorship is that the mentee is not at the level to wear the uniform and walk on the battlefield as a soldier. After completing ten weeks of being yelled at, cussed at, spit on, and etc., they find it hard to step up to the plate. Or, in some cases, the roles are reversed, and the mentor now has to walk as a mentee.

Role Reversal Tug of War

Did you know that there are soldiers in leadership positions that come out of uniform and step into the world without any structure presented to them? They soon realize that they got so comfortable following orders in the military that now, in society, things are not as structured. So, they find themselves answering to people younger than them. While some understand order, most do not, which leads these soldiers into a battlefield of chaos and disruption within themselves.

This is when a mentor, sergeant, and teacher must learn how to humble themselves repeatedly because as you teach, you are also learning. Sometimes people find themselves losing their identity and having to regain a positive consistent mindset to be led again by those in which they know nothing about them. This is why some veterans don't do well in a civilian world. They hunger for structure, order, and direct guidance that are set up to follow vision that leads to success. But what happens when they have no structure, order, or guidance? Without these initial points, you will never have a target and without a target, there is nowhere to aim!

Moving Through the Ranks

Moving through the ranks is not easy, but when you have a good leader and mentor guiding you, rising becomes easier. Wisdom kicks in as you start to pay attention to good leaders and bad leaders. When you follow bad leaders, you also become what you chose to follow. You will either be an effective mentor or just an influential one with no substance.

Sometimes the mentors you choose are not the ones that God chose for you. Or maybe they are only for a season, so it is your job to figure that out. In mentorship, you must provide the guidance needed to better your mentee and not enable them from becoming greater. Unlike the military, some mentors are afraid to correct those they are leading, especially in the church because of the fear of people leaving. But in the end those types of actions or should I say "non actions" are holding back everyone involved from pursuing future success as well as others coming forth, which is why they have a training in the military because they don't feed you a bottle; you have to get up and make your own plate!

- Your life demonstrates through lifestyle and not lip service! It is one thing to talk big about what you can do, but it's another thing to show just how big you can make others.
- You need a mentor that is touchable. They must be an overseer! But remember, there will always be flaws.

Give your mentor a pass because no one is perfect, but you will take on good and bad qualities of the one you choose to mentor you. Just like a soldier in the military will take on qualities of those training him or her, you as a mentee will also. No one is immune from flaws, so whoever you choose to be your mentor at some point, you will start to become like that person in one way or another. You must be willing to accept and adapt to the flaws of your mentor, taking on what you know is beneficial to you while also being mindful:

- Choose someone with wisdom and discernment.

Your mentor should be able to tell when something isn't right with you and talk to you about it. You want them to be able to pick it up without you having to always say anything. That is when you know that the two of you are connected. At some point, they must see you for who you are and be willing to accept you and put time and commitment into holding you accountable for your future and the future that God has prepared for you. A mentor can see things in you that you can't see in yourself and they are there to help pull them out. That is what makes the military so great because they see your faults, your weaknesses but choose to bring out the best in you!

Whether you know it or not, you are a soldier in two armies. Whether you are a soldier in the military, Army of the Lord, the classroom, on the court or field, and any area you serve in, you will always remain a soldier in the "Army of Mentorship". To be a successful mentor, you must have a desire to help develop other people.

Reflect on Your Experiences

Reflecting on your own experiences and sharing your failures is a huge part of creating that relationship that is needed to build trust and a willingness to pursue greater things even if failure may be an option. What we have built our lives on is understanding the freedom that we have gained because of mistakes made and battles won previously, so why not share your own with your mentee. Being a great mentor takes time, but you learn along the way, just as the mentee does. Think about turning an oven on and putting in a pizza. You know what the finished product will be if you follow the directions given on the box and keep a watchful eye on how the pizza is looking. Making sure that everything is rising as it should and when the timer goes off, you open the oven door and look inside. If the pizza is ready, you take it out, let it cool off, then you cut it and serve. Same thing we must do as a mentor. It is your job to keep watch, give direction, and make sure that when they come out of the oven (training) that they are ready!

Great teachers are usually the ones that are still wanting to learn themselves. Mentorship must be managed correctly and nurtured. Always remember that mentorship is not just a one-sided relationship, but it's a partnership.

"Do not go where the path may lead, go instead where there is no path and leave a trail."

— Ralph Waldo Emerson

CHAPTER 8

SOMEONE PAVED THE WAY

Just about every success story we hear about, a mentor paved the way even if some people claim they paved their own way and did it on their own. If the truth be told, someone was there to lay a foundation for them to walk upon, perhaps point them in a direction, give them a word of wisdom and put them on a path of success.

When we look at some influential preachers, we can immediately see the fruit on them endorsing someone who isn't well known. It may seem like their ministry took off overnight because of the endorsement. Doors of opportunity begin to open after years of being hidden. Being connected to the right person will pave the way because your floor is their ceiling. You aren't starting at the bottom as they might have. The stage has already been prepared. All you have to do now is walk on it. Through association, people will favor and support you.

Having these people connected in your life can be a game-changer, to help thrust or catapult the mentee into a whole new level: someone who pushes, encourages, challenges, and affirms you, all at the same time. I'm amazed at how one conversation, just one person taking a little extra time sharing a little advice can help set their feet on a path of great success. My friend, no one does it on their own! You saw something and while observing, you were able to take away something and make use of it somewhere on your journey.

Or perhaps what you heard someone else say, even if it's one word, it helped shape your destiny. While writing this chapter, so many things came to mind, my father being one. Having grown up in the south, or should I say, "deep south," he chose not to allow what happened in his childhood to affect him but to learn to push through it.

By brutal treatments of African Americans, the stories I heard inspired and motivated me all at the same time. So far, he taught me never to give up! Never allow the actions of others to hinder your hopes or abort your ambitions. My father was such a great example in teaching me never to let anyone label you. He would always say, "What they say about you doesn't make you who you are." Although this may not sound like a mentoring example, it was, and it is to this day.

So, I would have to disagree that you have gotten to where you are by yourself. So please, before we use the words: "self-made millionaires or billionaires," "self-made businessman or women," or "you made it to the top without anyone's help or assistance," we should check those statements.

- Someone paved the way…
- Someone opened a door for you…
- Someone spoke up for you…
- Someone walked you through it…

I'm thankful for the pioneers who blazed the trail for me. Also, I'm grateful for those who encouraged me along the way. I wouldn't be where I am or who I am if it wasn't for those who went before me to pave the way.

"You teach what you know…but impart who you are."

— Jack Frost

CHAPTER 9

CULTIVATING THE LEGACY

For a family, you must cultivate the home. For a Christian, you must cultivate the mind, body, and spirit. For a farmer, you must cultivate the crops, but for a legacy, you must cultivate the blood line! Just as the crops need to be tilled, your attention, in the same way, needs to be just as focused on nurturing and building up your family for growth and ownership. So, when you leave, you will leave a "crop rotation" legacy to not just produce in their lives but the future generations to come.

Crop rotation is a practice of growing a series of different types of crops in the same area but just in sequenced seasons. Just like the lives from one generation to the next living and producing a harvest passing on the wisdom of the old while living in expectation of the young. There are roots still yet to come forth. There are crops still yet to plant! Every day you work towards building your legacy from underneath the ground first (which is within), making your family strong just by shaping the very foundation and soil. They will come to know and being present constantly pouring nutrients into them that will continually improve the structure and the precision of their placement in this world.

Parents, grandparents, aunts, and uncles are the greatest influential mentors that you will ever have in your life. Without them being in a mentee role at some point in their life, they would never be in the position now to produce a lasting legacy for you. They had to go through some things, learn some very hard life lessons, learned how to work hard for everything that they earned, gaining knowledge and wisdom from mistakes made and victories won to get you where you need to be, but the legacy that is left is not always physical.

Joshua 4:6-7 states, "When your children ask in time to come, saying, 'What do these stones mean to you?' then you shall answer them that the waters of the Jordan were cut off before the ark of the covenant of the Lord; when it crossed over the Jordan, the waters of the Jordan were cut off. And these stones shall be for a memorial to the children of Israel forever."

The foundation in which you frame your legacy will be the determining factor of extent of the inheritance. A great mentor of mine and family member has set the foundation for leaving a lasting legacy for our family. Just as the Israelites were instructed from the middle of the Jordan to set stones up as a memorial of God's faithfulness, He also taught us to guard our relationship with Jesus Christ. Also, remember to keep grabbing the stones continually building the memorial of faithfulness and surety in Him that His word is stamped with our salvation.

Some people base legacies on superficial things of this earth, but there is also the legacy of the everlasting things of heaven. A godly inheritance is much more valuable to the one who has lived this life. But for the young, it is something that needs to be learned.

In interviewing mentors within families, there are two regrets spoken of the most. First, the lack of time spent with their own children due to being gone too much. Secondly, it was the lack of mentoring those outside the home due to working and only spending time with the ones within the walls. No outside cultivating was able to be manifested from the root, because it was only the fruit that had a chance to survive. In the discussion, meeting the needs of other families was so great that the needs at home were not being met. As a result, it led to more outside influence, making the chance to cultivate the legacy that much harder from within.

Ask yourself these questions. What do you want now compared to what your family may need later? What are your vision and your goals for your family? What kind of legacy do you want to leave behind? Think about the people in your life right now. If you were to leave here tomorrow, what would you leave them with? You only get one try, and time is something that we do not get back. Proverbs 13:22 says, "A good man leaves an inheritance to his children's children." An inheritance is never limited to just money. When you invest godly character in the hearts of those in your home and start cultivating financial wisdom in the minds of your children, you are teaching them how to earn money the right way. Also, you are helping them to build a lasting foundation. Eventually, integrity and wisdom are built, ensuring that whatever you leave financially, physically, and spiritually will last and continue to live even after you are gone. You must cultivate your vision by joining them in spirit and truth. The more you pray with your family, the less tilling that you will have to do because the more you pray, the closer you are to God, and the closer you are to God, the closest your harvest will always remain.

Deuteronomy 11:19 states, "Teach them to your children. Talk about them when you are at home and when you are on the road, when you are going to bed and when you are getting up."

"Wisdom and understanding can only become the possession of individual men by traveling the old road of observation, attention, perseverance, and industry."

— Samuel Smiles

CHAPTER 10

THE ROLE OF A MENTEE

A mentee must perform several roles. Mentoring is a partnership between two individuals: the mentor and the mentee. In considering the roles of the mentor, he or she must wear many hats throughout the process. As a mentor, they are to take the lead in the relationship at least initially, but a mentee must also perform several roles.

1. The mentee is the student who needs to absorb the mentor's knowledge and have the ambition and desire to know what to do with this knowledge.
2. A mentee is a gauge to measure how interactive the connection between the mentor and themselves.
3. Mentees need to pray for their mentors. They don't know what warfare their leader is going through. Also, praying for people will place the love of God in our hearts so there will be no room for jealousy when doors start to open for leadership.
4. Mentees need to serve their mentors to take a burden off them. As they serve underneath leadership, they qualified for the double portion anointing.

5. Mentees need to sow into their mentors. You sow into a person's vision when you believe in it. You sow into their ministry so they can do more for the Kingdom.
6. Mentees are to support their mentors by attending conferences, trainings, and sharing their content on social media.

The mentor may share with a mentee or protégé information about his or her own career path as well as provide guidance, motivation, emotional support, and role modeling.

The mentor may help with exploring careers, setting goals, developing contacts, and identifying resources. Here are some basic characteristics the ideal mentee:

- Eagerness to learn
- Ability and willingness to work as a team player
- Patience
- Risk-taker
- Positive attitude
- Humility
- Supportive
- Great listener
- Faithful

As a student, the mentee needs to practice and demonstrate what has been learned.

1) The mentee must be willing to listen and respect the opportunities that are afforded to them.

Be very careful not to interrupt, unless you need clarity, be sure to ask good questions and have a purpose for your questions and prepare the goals and objectives you have for your career. Remain teachable because you are there to learn and receive something from your mentor's life.

2) Ask questions concerning your vision, your goals, plans, and strategies.

The more specific you can be, the easier it will be for your mentor to help you. Don't be afraid to ask for feedback, although the response might be difficult to hear, it is critical to your spiritual growth and development. Asking questions shows your eagerness to learn and that you value your leader's time by pulling on the anointing that they carry.

3) Stay open to new ideas and suggestions and don't get offended.

Rather than giving feedback, thank your mentor for taking a risk to be honest with you. You must remember if your mentor was not invested in you, they would not take the risk. Honest feedback gives you the opportunity to improve yourself and help you move forward in fulfilling and reaching your potential. Remember, your mentor may see something that you aren't seeing.

4) Stay faithful and dependable

You are serving unto God, not men, so you want to walk in a spirit of excellence. Let your word be true and keep all your promises. You are there to make your leader's job easier, and in return, they can have more time to pour into you and do other great exploits. Treat your leader's assignment as you would your own.

Mentors provide information and knowledge as Benjamin Franklin said, "Tell me and I'll forget, teach me and I'll remember, invade me and I'll learn." While speaking to a very successful businessman when starting, out he had no idea what all it involved running a business. Including making a business run, bridging, handling daily operations, running a marketing campaign, but having a mentor right from the start, he was able to tap into wealth and knowledge and brought me up to speed faster and shortened that learning curve. Countless numbers of interviewees all said the same thing. They all were so very thankful for having a mentor to help groom, direct, and guide them along the way. Quality mentoring greatly enhances students' chances for success.

"Mentoring is a two-way street. The mentor gets wiser while mentoring and the mentee gains knowledge through his/her mentor."

— Marisol Gonzalez

CHAPTER 11

MENTORSHIP PROVIDES A COVERING

The importance of a spiritual covering has been mentioned in previous chapters showing just how many roles a mentor plays in just one life. While interviewing a well-known leader in the Christian faith, he really emphasized the importance of a covering for accountability. Everyone needs checks and balances. He was so busy doing ministry traveling full time, a schedule always on the go, that he neglected his family. It caused major problems in his marriage, which led to a divorce. After listening to wise counseling and allowing his mentor to speak wisdom in this matter, the couple was reunited. To this day, they are doing well because of the spiritual covering. My friend, no one needs to be out there without a spiritual covering!

I wonder how many marriages would be saved today if only we had wise men and women that we were accountable to that would help lead and guide us through those difficult times. Just as simple as spending time with family uninterrupted, focusing on the family and making them a priority holds much value. What if you go out and win the world and lose your family, what have you really gained? Not much. You lose more than you gained in the long run, which is why having a mentor, a spiritual covering, is a blessing that will save you more times than none.

Mentors see the changes that we need to make and the things that we need to improve in our own lives, even the ones we can't see. Mentors have a way of seeing more of our faults than we would like them to, but if it's the only way to grow, then we must listen. Mentors will tell you exactly how it is instead of downplaying your weakness, they will provide constructive criticism to help you see things in yourself that you haven't recognized. Mentors are not there to stroke your ego, but to build greatness in you to withstand.

Mentors will also stimulate your personal growth. It is not the mentor creating the mentee in their own image but allowing the opportunity to create themselves. Mentors set goals for you and then sit back and watch you accomplish them. Then they sit you down and tell you what he/she observed through the process, which involves them telling you what to keep, what to throw out, what to continue doing, or what doesn't work for you.

Mentors offer encouragement that helps keep us going. Oprah Winfrey stated, "A mentor is someone who allows you to see the hope inside yourself." They are there no matter what, through the good, the bad, and the ugly. They never give up on you even when you give up on yourself. They won't let you stop. Mentors keep you motivated and full of confidence.

Mentors are also disciplinaries that help create boundaries to keep you from distraction. We must focus on mentors. Years ago, one of the top revivalists in the country committed adultery and divorced his wife. His sins halted the international revival that was occurring. He repented for his sins and married his mistress. He sat down from ministry for a while because that was the advice of the mentors around him. They held this minister accountable and vouched when he was ready to start ministering after they made sure he had a contrite spirit and living a holy life. When something occurs, people need to be able to go to our leadership because they are the voices that have permission to correct us if we go astray.

One of my friends mentioned the fact of buying another building. After consulting with a mentor, he realized it was the right thing to do, but the wrong time to do it. Wisdom tells us that timing is everything. The Word of God tells us before you build or buy, sit down first, and count the cost. There are so many operating out of season. Ecclesiastes 3:1 says, "To everything, there is a season," and a wise, trusted counselor has a way of understanding the timing of God.

I have seen a lot of people start many projects but never complete them, but when the Lord has provided wisdom through someone who has gone through the same things, now my mistakes today will minister to you tomorrow.

"The road less traveled tends to be the roughest because not many have had to conquer it, but the greatness of those that have made it to the end is that they live to tell it."

— Amber M. Brown

CHAPTER 12

FATHERS OF THE FAITH

Where are they? Many are leaving us, and many have fallen asleep. Apostle Paul stated, "For we have many instructors but very few fathers." This generation is suffering from the lack of fatherhood naturally and spiritually. The fathers of faith hold a standard of holiness and hold us accountable. They were builders not only of buildings, but they were builders of life, value, stability, integrity, righteousness, and the foundation of faith. When we came along, we were taught to honor the fathers of the faith. Not only looking up to them, but we also look to them for wisdom and understanding. The old gray heads are missing in the room. They are exiting one by one. They kept us grounded, honest, reaching up and reaching out to God. They trained, instructed, and rebuked us often. Then they would encourage us. Many times, they would cut you open and then sew you back up again. But they earned the right to do so. They spoke into our lives. They mantled, motivated, and helped manage us. Then they ministered to us.

God said, "I call you young men because you're strong and you overcome the wicked. Young one I call you for war, but father I called you for wisdom, counsel, and to help bring balance." Now we have many leaders who are attending sheep, protecting sheep, instead of training soldiers. Ephesians 4:11-12 says, "And he himself gave some apostles, some prophets, some pastors, some evangelists, some teachers." Why? For the equipping of the saints, for the work of the ministry, and for the edifying of the Body of Christ. So, in this generation, many are reigning but very few are training! I see minor mistakes are being made, but on the other hand, I see major mistakes also being made. Of course, we made our share of them, but the father of the faith was there to correct and direct us when we veered off the path of purpose. Believe it or not, we welcomed discipline because in the long run or short run, it made us better, as individuals and leaders, but this generation doesn't receive correction very well. However, you must understand that correction and discipline are all part of our development. What this generation thinks are punishments; the others know it's a process. I am very thankful for the fathers of faith, who help lead, guide, guard, ground, and encourage me through difficult times, especially when it was hard to navigate certain situations.

We must realize that a spiritual father isn't our friend, but they are here to tell us the truth even when it hurts. They don't care how well you can preach, pray, or prophesy. They don't exist to flatter your ego, and they don't look at you as a dollar sign. They are concerned about your purpose, and they are making their investment as they pour into your life. A spiritual father is a covenant relationship.

A spiritual father isn't jealous of you. They will open up doors and opportunities as they recommend you. There's no need to compete with one another because as your spiritual father is elevated, then so are you. He can give you more revelation, and as you are faithful to serve overtime, more exposure for your ministry will happen. They won't be envious when you get more speaking engagements or make more money. When he goes up, you go up because he is pulling you higher. Just as a parent in the natural wants their children to be better than them, so does a spiritual parent.

A spiritual father loves you and wants the best for you. They will sacrifice to make sure that you succeed if needed. They will pray you through the warfare and will be by your side. They value your relationship and long to fellowship with you. They can be gentle at times but don't mind correcting if needed. They aren't controlling, manipulating, or oppressing. They will lead by example so you can follow in their footsteps. They will make sure that you can have access to them. A person is not your spiritual parent if you can never contact them. They will make sure that you have their personal number, and you will have a level of intimacy with them that the people on the outside don't have.

My biological father raised ten children and he believed in training. Being raised on a farm helped some things to come naturally to me because I use many of those same principles that we have applied in the spiritual realm. But now so many of those resources are lacking. We've had many to leave us without tapping into their gifts, talents, anointings, and teachings. So, we are now suffering because of a lack of guidance, guarding, and directing.

"The two most important days in your life are the day you were born and the day you find out why."

— Mark Twain

CHAPTER 13

THE GREATEST MENTOR OF THEM ALL

Jesus was the greatest mentor of them all. He led so we could follow. He said if any man comes after me, let him deny himself and take up his cross and follow me daily (Matthew 16:24). Jesus imparted wisdom and knowledge through His words and actions. He showed his disciples that the values of the kingdom are different from the values of the world. Jesus also taught his disciples that they should be servants. He demonstrated the behavior that He wanted them to have by first doing it themselves. Jesus brought them close to train, mentor, and test them. That's what a good mentor does.

Jesus taught his followers how to pray, which will sustain our ministries over time. Jesus withdrew Himself from the crowd to go pray multiple times. Mentees can look at his behavior and gain the importance of prayer. Jesus prayed for his crucifiers and us (John 17). As we follow Christ's example, we learn how to pray through difficult situations.

Jesus taught his mentees to fast as they look at what he endured in the wilderness (Luke 4). When the enemy tempts us, fasting will help us to resist him and not fall into sin. Jesus provided a great example of denying self, so we don't get caught in pitfalls such as riches and fame. He instilled into His mentees' determination during the hardships, living a holy life, and destroying the works of the devil (1 John 3:8).

Jesus demonstrated how to love and accept people that were rejected. For instance, he stopped the woman that was caught in adultery from being stoned (John 8) and spoke to the Samaritan woman at the well (John 4). His mentees experienced His compassion on the multitude that led to the crowd of 5000 being fed (Matthew 14:13-21). Jesus is the best mentor because He is the reason for our faith, and when we keep our eyes on Him, we can't go wrong.

The mentor must serve as a model and a trusted listener. Mentors depend on the Holy Spirit to provide insight so he or she can, in return, pass it on to the mentee. Later, I will discuss the importance of the mentee's submission and his or her willingness to listen to the wisdom and instruction of the mentor.

The Apostle Paul is one of our best examples of being mentored and then, in return, mentoring others. Paul speaks about how mentoring is very simple, "Follow my example as I follow Christ (1 Corinthians 11:1)." Whatever you have learned of me or seen in me, put it into practice (Philippians 4:9). Paul is saying, "Let me mentor you. Let me be your model." That's why he encourages them. Expect others to follow their example. They must be wholeheartedly committed to following Christ. Not only Jesus and Apostle Paul but the elders in the church as well.

The Apostle Peter commands us to be examples to the flock (1 Peter 5:3) and Paul explains to the elders at Ephesus, you know how I lived the whole time I was with you. In other words, Paul said, "I showed you now you show others." That's what mentoring is all about, always remembering how others helped, encouraged, and strengthened you. Even how others rescued you, now in return, help, strengthen, and encourage others. From generation to generation, we must continue mentorship.

None of us will fully become all that God has created us to be unless we have a mentor by our side. If you're reading this book and you've suffered from the lack of a mentor, I would like to encourage you to pray and ask God to put the right person or persons in your path. Although the term mentor is not Biblical, The Bible speaks to Christians in terms of discipleship. From a secular standpoint, we hear of programs like Big Brothers Big Sisters of America, but the ultimate source of true-life transformation is the Holy Spirit plus the Word of God, skillfully and prayerfully utilized by those called as mentors within the Body of Christ. The foundation concept of mentoring is found in the following passage. God provided a Biblical format of mentoring within the family to ensure that faith in the one true and living God would be passed on from generation to generation. Deuteronomy 6:4-9 states, "Hear, O Israel: The Lord our God, the Lord is one. Love the Lord your God with all your heart and with all your soul and with all your strength. These commandments that I give you today are to be on your hearts. Impress them on your children. Talk about them when you sit at home and when you walk along the road, when you lie down and when you get up. Tie them as symbols on your hands and bind them on your foreheads. Write them on the doorframes of your houses and on your gates."

Every entry point of your life, in the New Testament, Jesus extended to the community!

Matthew 22:36-40 says, "Teacher, which is the greatest commandment in the Law?" Jesus replied, "Love the Lord your God with all your heart and with all your soul and with all your mind. This is the first and greatest commandment. And the second is like it. Love your neighbor as yourself." So, it's all about developing relationships. Raising up disciples, mentoring, and encouraging others.

"Give a man a fish and you feed him for a day; teach a man to fish and you feed him for a lifetime."

— Maimonides

CHAPTER 14

THE JETHRO PRINCIPLE

The Jethro Principle occurs when Jethro mentored his son-in-law, Moses (Exodus 18:1). Now Jethro, the Priest of Midian and the father-in-law of Moses, heard of everything God had done for Moses and His people in Israel. He also heard of how the Lord brought the children of Israel out of Egypt. Moses began to tell of how God delivered them from the hands of bondage out of Pharaoh's hand, but then something happened after the burnt offering and other sacrifices were made. Aaron and some of the elders came to eat a meal with Moses in the presence of God and his father-in-law, Jethro.

- But the next day, Moses took his seat to judge and to serve as the people stood around him from the morning until evening (Exodus 18:13).
- When his father-in-law Jethro saw all that Moses was doing for the people, he began to question him. What are you doing for the people? Why are you sitting alone judging all these people that's standing around you day and night, morning until evening (Exodus 18:14)?
- Moses' reply was because the people come to me to seek God's will. When they have a dispute, it's brought to me. I decide between the parties and inform them of God's

decrees and instructions. Remember, Moses is just doing what he feels is right. He believes he's doing God's will, but his mentor observes his ministry. "Moses, what you're doing is not good! If you continue to do what you're doing," he said, "You and the people shall wear away, then you're going to wear yourself out." Why? Because the work is too heavy for you to do it alone. Moses, you need some help. He's simply reciting the problem, but Moses is not angry or upset at this point, he's doing the best he can (Exodus 18:15).

Now wisdom speaks up. This shows how it's important to listen to voices of experience. Jethro now summons a solution. Listen now to me. I will give you advice and may God be with you.

"Moses, you must be the people's representatives before God and bring their disputes to Him and not yourself." He told him what to do and advised him on how to do it. Moses teaches them the decrees, laws, and instructions. He shows them the way they ought to live and how they are to behave. Jethro said to Moses, "Select capable men from all the people: men who fear God, trustworthy, hate dishonesty, and dishonest gain. Appoint these capable men over thousands, hundreds, fifties, and tens. Have them help you always serve as judges for the people, but make sure they bring all the difficult staff or weighty matters to you. The simple cases they can judge or handle themselves." But why, Jethro? So, Moses can last longer. They will make the load lighter.

There are so many over-loaded leaders who really need to read this passage in the Bible and get their hands on this book. It will lighten the load of leadership. They will last longer in ministry, and as a CEO or president of a corporation. Jethro served as a positive mentor in Moses's life and as a result, it prevented burn out. He was able to do his job plus help and encourage the people. We need mentors who are passionate about helping leaders and those who will show acts of care, compassion and respect. But at the same time, not be afraid to enter a respectful, honest dialogue to further build trust. His advice helped take the pressure off him, plus he regained his focus, strength, and wisdom. Because Jethro used the right approach, Moses benefited from his wisdom. Jethro celebrated Moses and encouraged him first. Then he observed his duties, gave him sound advice, and the rest is history.

"**Mentoring is a brain to pick, an ear to listen, and a push in the right direction.**"

— John C. Crosby

CHAPTER 15

MENTORSHIP THROUGH A BOOK

Some of the best mentors in the world are no longer with us, but their books will carry centuries of knowledge and wisdom for generations to come. If you were to go up to ten people and ask them about their mentor, at least half of them would tell you that their mentor would be found in a book. Jim Rohn once said, "You are the average of the five people you spend the most time with." So, out of the five people you spend the most time with, would one of those be found in a book?

The Bible is a great example of a mentor being found in a book. From beginning to end, there are stories filled with different people who have been through different things but have learned and shared wisdom through the process that will charge you, challenge you, and motivate you for the development and shaping of your present and your future. Reading the Bible can change you and get you moving in the right direction without anyone being present around you. The knowledge, revelation, experience, and wisdom of another individual that has already read the chapter that you are just now starting can also be your guide while moving through this thing called mentorship.

What books have had the most influence on you and why? Think about the last book you read. Write down what you learned from that book and how it was helpful in guiding and mentoring you for the future. There are many different types of mentors out there, but depending upon who you are and what you need will strongly determine the choice of book you choose to read. Sometimes even stepping away from the usual and spending quality time with a mentor that you are unfamiliar with may open your eyes to seeing things from a different perspective. Some books on your bookshelf should be different so that your mind can stay open to receiving and learning from different avenues and different ways of life.

A mentor from a book may not be present, but by reading their words and visualizing your life in connection with theirs welcomes a powerful impact of growth and change in a moment that is no one else's but yours. That is your time to study their habits, learn from their mistakes, and determine their strategies of living a successful life. You may find that there are things already written in a book by a mentor just waiting on you to receive that you may never learn from someone in your lifetime of knowing. The ultimate mentor will bring a hunger out of you for more. Until you find that mentor in your life, you must search for him/her in that bookshelf called mentors. When you least expect it, God will place a person in your life who has been chosen specifically to push you into greatness. Hopefully, by learning from your mentors found in your books, you will be more prepared when you meet them. It is never too late or too early to start preparing. We should always be living in preparation!

Martin Luther King Jr. once said, "Human progress is neither automatic nor inevitable. Every step toward the goal of justice requires sacrifice, suffering, and struggle; the tireless exertions and passionate concern of dedicated individuals." Those dedicated individuals are your mentors! They show us how to go through suffering and still have hope for the future. They teach us what true sacrifice is all about. They guide us through their struggles so that we, in hopes, will not make the same mistakes. It was mentors like Howard Thurman, Mordecai Johnson, and Bayard Rustin, who encouraged Dr. Martin Luther King Jr.

Even Benjamin Mays is known to be one of Dr. Martin Luther King Jr.'s greatest mentors who helped him learn about the history of our nation. You see, Dr. King had many mentors around him, but not all of them were visible. Some of them were only found in books for a certain time. That is the great thing about that bookshelf called mentors because at any time, you can pick them up, learn from them, and then put them back until their wisdom is needed again. You may not need every word given at that particular time, but sooner or later, you will need that book again. That mentor will spark something within you at just the right time that will cause them to come alive in you and allow their legacy to be carried through you.

Howard Thurman is one of the greatest mentors of all time and the best moments of his mentoring you will find in his books. Thurman once said, "Don't ask what the world needs. Ask what makes you come alive and go do it because what the world needs are people who have come alive."

"When a leader fails to address a problem, the problem is no longer the problem. The problem is the leader."

—Craig Groeschel

CHAPTER 16

OUT OF ORDER

One of the most challenging areas to deal with when it comes to mentorship is getting an understanding of knowing truly what lane yours is to walk in. No one ever wants to live a life that was never meant for them. It just won't work! Just as you cannot walk in other's shoes, you cannot live another's life and think that it will work out the same for you. Your individual walk is a daily decision. Every day you must decide to be in line and in order with God for your own life and to not be out of design with His plan for you. This world was created and designed with a plan and a purpose for you.

Have you ever been told to "stay in your lane"? Yes, we hear it and say it all the time. But to truly know your lane, you must know who you are and continue to learn who you are and what your job is! People change and grow daily. Everyone has been given a gift in a certain area of life that will only benefit and bless you if you pursue THAT GIFT. You know the saying that "even if they start with you, they may not always finish with you." Well, that is because some people lose themselves along the way. Some people even change for the better. In other cases, people start walking in a lane that they were never meant to walk, which is why having the right mentee and the right mentor is so important.

Jude 1:6 states, "Even the angels in knowing who they were meant to serve and what job description they were given, did not stay within their own position of authority. But left their dwelling, and because of that, they are still chained under darkness until the day of judgment."

What the angels didn't realize was that they were one decision away from eternal order or eternal chaos! You see, the angels of God veered off track because they chose to follow a leader who changed lanes! A leader who allowed pride and greed to get in the way. Who allowed power and authority to overtake the very hearts of those under him, which led to their downfall! Now instead of mentorship of eternal life through God, growth and development, those angels are now so-called mentees of a mentor who will spend an eternity in hell.

They followed the wrong person, which led them down the wrong path causing them NOT to stay in their lane. Instead of staying in their own lane with God who created them, they chose to follow guidance from an angel who wanted more power and authority than his Creator. Because of that, he decided to act in a position that was never meant for him! Are you finding yourself in a position that you know was never meant for you?

If so, today is the day to get back on track and get back in your lane. This happens more times than we can count. Just because one person gets off track it doesn't mean that you should too. Even though a mentee is the one learning and being trained, you still have to choose righteousness. Not every mentor is going to be the right kind of mentor for you, and the angels are a great example of what happens when you follow the wrong people.

We have two primary questions while in mentorship. Are you as a mentee going to operate in order and respect your mentor and humble yourself to be taught? And are you as a mentor going to live, teach, and pour into another individual while staying in order with God? There are so many people that will not humble themselves under a mentor because they believe that they don't need one. Some mentors are operating in a headship position that was never given to them in the first place.

A mentee is out of order when they disrespect their mentors. A mentee should address their mentor by their title if they have one instead of their first name because they don't want to get too familiar. When that occurs, then they will start to view the relationship differently. A mentee should watch how they talk to their mentors because it isn't a friendship but mentorship. Familiarity breeds content and the mentee stops receiving advice from the mentor. Anything that is not with the vision is division.

Mentees are out of order when they are unfaithful. Can your mentor depend on you to do what you promised? Will you mess up the flow because you are out of position? Will you make others' jobs harder because you bailed out at the last minute? Things will happen, but consistency is vital. If you are always late, never show up, and unreliable, that says something about your character and that you don't value the mentorship.

A mentee is out of order when boundaries are crossed. Every healthy relationship needs barriers. If the mentor hasn't given you permission for your opinion, then it doesn't need to be stated. Who is mentoring who? To reiterate, your mentor isn't your homegirl or your homeboy. Stay out of their marriage and personal affairs unless the circumstance presents otherwise. Don't get jealous when you see your mentor around other leaders and not with you. Remember, you can't have them all to yourself because they are called to equip others.

When we do not know who we are or what we are supposed to be doing in this world, we get lost. When we get lost, we find ourselves seeking for things and people that were never meant to come into our lives. Therefore, it is vital in a mentorship relationship for both people to learn what role they play, not only in each other's lives, but in teaching and following as an individual.

Also, from another angle, you could start mentoring in one area. As you start learning giftings and growing, you may turn and go another route. Even as a mentee, you may be in training and come across a project that gets you to open up more and show another side of you and that maybe you didn't even know about yourself. So, pay attention to these things. You may start being mentored in sports but realize that you have a gift of writing. The same mentor that trains you in sports may not be the same mentor that teaches you the techniques of writing, but that doesn't mean that you can't start walking in that lane.

God created you for a specific purpose. If you do not know who you are or what that purpose is, then it is time for you to find out! Pray about it and walk in obedience to His Word and you will never find yourself operating out of order.

It was only when the angels didn't stay in their lane and chose to walk out of order with God that they had a great fall! It was only when Adam and Eve didn't stay in their lane and chose to walk out of order with God that they had a great fall!

"In order to be a mentor, and an effective one, one must care. You must care. You don't have to know how many square miles are in Idaho. You don't need to know what the chemical makeup of chemistry is, or of blood or water. Know what you know and care about the person. Care about what you know. Care about the person you're sharing with."

— Maya Angelou

CHAPTER 17

DON'T UNDERESTIMATE DISTRACTIONS

How many times do your plans change throughout the day? It's like you have everything already planned out, but it seems like there is always something that happens to cause you to get distracted. Never underestimate a distraction! Even one distraction can mess up your entire day if you let it. So, how come some days you continue knocking out your plans and going with the flow while other days a distraction can stop you right in your tracks? It is because of your mindset, which must be trained! If you are not prepared to handle yourself or have not been taught how to flow in life regardless of what comes your way, distractions can be devastating to your growth. If you do not have the tools and resources to prevent distractions from moving you out of position, then mentorship is a needed practice for you.

Even when there are distractions around you, you can still choose how to react to those distractions. Have you ever watched a horse compete while racing? If you haven't, you need to go watch a race sometime or look it up on YouTube. Sometimes the horses can get distracted by the other horses in the race, so the trainers put blinkers or "blinders" on them so that during the race, their only option is to look straight ahead of them. The eyes of the horse stay focused in one direction and never looks to the left or the right. That is the mindset a mentee must have to build a strong foundation for mentorship. If the mentor is always pouring into you, but you are always distracted and not using what they are giving to you, then really, you have already lost the race.

A mentor-mentee relationship is two-fold and they shouldn't be distracted when they are talking to each other. When someone is always interrupted by phone calls, emails, or people walking by when in a session with you, then they may not be actively listening. Shutting out the distractions makes the other person feel like they are important. During the conversation, both parties need to focus, ask questions, reflect on answers, and have time to process the information.

Repeat after me, "I will stay focused on what is ahead of me and not get distracted by other things or people to the left of me, to the right of me, those coming up behind me, or even those already ahead of me. I choose this day to be led in the direction I need to go by the person specifically chosen by God to walk in the purpose of my life." The Bible tells us that our steps are ordered by the Lord, but even so, God doesn't promise that we will never get to our goals without distractions, especially in mentorship.

Some people don't want you to do well because they haven't done well, but you are going to choose not to be that type of person. Whatever they can do to try to stop your purpose moving forward, trust me, they will try, but you cannot get distracted by things or people. We don't have much time. Every day matters and is another step towards greatness, but without a mentor, what should take you 11 days will end up taking you 40 years.

The Bible teaches us the importance of leadership and listening to those who have walked this life before you. Exodus 13 speaks of a situation where a distraction ends up costing many more than what they should have lost, and that was the victory in the Promised Land. What should have been an eleven-day journey in the wilderness ended up lasting forty years! Just imagine living a life of one mess up, arrest, and accident after the other, living every day feeling like it was just as the last. All you needed was a mentor to help pull you out of that kind of life and push you into the life that you've always wanted. The Israelites could have had that, but they chose to complain and not listen to Moses, and because of that, it cost them years of their life. Don't let that be you! Don't allow distractions to hold you back from your Promised Land. Choose mentorship and allow yourself to reach your goals in less time because you received guidance and discipline along the way.

> "By prevailing over all obstacles and distractions, one may unfailing arrive at his chosen goal or destination."
>
> — **Christopher Columbus**

CHAPTER 18

MENTORING MOMENTS

I believe what you're about to read will inspire, encourage, and challenge you all together. Maybe you feel like you could never be a mentor, well I disagree. Everyone can mentor in some capacity. When you see a child in need of guidance, help, encouragement, direction, or correction, just by taking the time to speak to them can be life-changing.

If they value your voice for them, it could be a voice of victory. SEIZE THE MOMENT and mentor them by giving:

1. Sound wisdom
2. Recommending a book
3. Encouraging them in their studies
4. Making yourself a resource for them by showing them or exposing them to greatness
5. Show your concern by spending quality time with them
6. Don't forget to listen to them
7. Accept where your mentees are and work with them to improve
8. Be honest

SHAKING HANDS WITH WISDOM

<u>Are you ready to mentor? Consider the following:</u>

1. You know that you are ready to mentor when you have accomplishments or skilled in your craft.
2. You feel that you have the wisdom to impart in others that want to go where you have already been.
3. Your motives are right concerning others and you want them to succeed.
4. You can help your mentee set goals and offer guidance so they can achieve them.
5. You don't want to see others make the same mistakes you have made and you can easily recognize it.
6. You learned the lesson from your own failures and you are willing to teach others the same.
7. You are compassionate about seeing the growth of others.
8. You will dedicate time to talk and spend time with others.
9. You have great listening skills and you will ask the right questions to help others get the best results.
10. You don't mind sharing your secrets or revelation that you gained.
11. You have been or currently being mentored.

I believe we will be afforded many opportunities to make a difference in the lives of others. The only question is, are you ready to take that step?

It all begins in 1 Kings 3. Solomon loved the Lord and sacrificed regularly. Once while he was sacrificing, the Lord appeared to him, "What do you want Solomon (1 Kings 3:5)?" We read his answer, "Give your servant, therefore, an understanding mind, (heart) to govern your people that I may discern between good and evil (1 Kings 3:9)." God heard this and answered Solomon's prayer, and made him the wisest person that ever lived. In a very interesting twist, God then says because you didn't ask for wealth, a long life, or your enemies' heads, I'm going to grant it to you, and Solomon reigned another 40 years.

He was legendary in many ways, especially for his wisdom. People would come from other countries to seek out Solomon, including the Queen of Sheba. He spoke 3,000 Proverbs and made 1,005 songs. He built the temple, and he centralized worship for Jerusalem.

Israel became very prosperous under Solomon's leadership. God gave him such wisdom that in the Bible, two mothers were brought to him, both claiming the same baby. But it was Solomon's wisdom that brought relief to the real mother. Solomon called for a sword and commanded the baby to be cut in half. One of the ladies agreed to take half the child, but the real mother screamed out, "Don't harm the baby. Give it to the other woman." So, Solomon hears the cry of the real mother then says, "Take your child and go home," because no real mother wants to see harm or hurt come to their child.

Now the sad part is the man who was granted wisdom now dies a fool! Like a lot of leaders, Solomon started strong but ended weak. Solomon was told not to marry strange women or the daughters of foreign kings, but he didn't listen. He also used forced labor and heavy taxation to accomplish his conquest and his building programs. Now, you are slowly seeing Solomon's life going downhill. We see quickly that the once wise man is now becoming a fool.

Then Solomon builds temples to these foreign gods. While once giving wisdom to others now we do not see him applying any to himself, which is sad. He had it all: wealth, power, and wisdom.

Just Listen Wisdom is Speaking

Solomon's son Rehoboam is now the successor after Solomon's reign for 40 years. Solomon was known for his wisdom, now his son has big shoes to fill. He would have to prove if he's wise enough to solve a problem. The Israelites felt oppressed and they sent representatives to tell Rehoboam what they wanted him to do. "Your fathers made our yoke harsh, but if you make the hard service of your father easier, just lighten the heavy yoke you put on the people, they will serve you." Just lighten up a little (2 Chronicles 10:3-4).

Rehoboam had a difficult choice to make. If he did what the people wanted, he and his family and those in the palace, might have to live without the luxuries of life for a while, which is something they had become accustomed to. However, if he refused the people's request, they might rebel against him. So, what did he do? He first talked with the older men who had helped his father. They gave him good wisdom and told him to listen to the people. Then Rehoboam spoke to those of his own age, which by the way, was a terrible mistake because they didn't have any experience. So, he decided to treat the people harshly and he told them that he would make their yoke harder and add to it. "My father made your yoke heavy; I will make it even heavier. My father scourged you with whips; I will scourge you with scorpions (2 Chronicles 10:6-14)."

Can you see the wisdom in this? We have many older saints who have served Jehovah for many, many years who can help us make good decisions if we listen.

Job 12:12 says,"Is not wisdom found among the aged? Does not long-life bring understanding?"

If I'm going to trust your direction, it will be because you've traveled this road before!

If you tell me this way will work, it will be because you've tried it before!

No one wants to be assigned to a tour guide that doesn't know the course. While traveling to third world countries, we were told to stay close to our guide, to listen to them, and to not veer off alone.

Our lives will be richer...

Our paths will shine brighter...

Only if we submit to the VOICE OF WISDOM!

"A mentor can say the right words to someone at exactly the right moment they need to hear it. And it can be life-changing."

— Kevin Spacey

CHAPTER 19

OPEN BOOK

Paul's mentoring ministry methods were somewhat different, but on the other hand, maybe not. Paul wasn't afraid to open up his life to his young protégé's. This is a very interesting concept. Paul realized that programs don't train people; people train people. So, Paul's method of mentoring, I feel, was one of the best because we should lead by example. We live in a society that will tell you, "Do as I say. Don't do as I do." Well, my friend, that's not Paul's approach. "Follow me as I follow Christ." Paul said, "Follow my example as I follow the example of Christ."

Later, Paul encourages Timothy, "Don't let anyone despise or look down on your youth but set an example for the believers in speech, life, love, faith, and purity (1 Timothy 4:1)." Paul keeps us honest and on our toes in his teaching and especially this challenge. Paul said our lives must reflect Christ in every way if we're going to impact this next generation.

Remember living as an open example, we must learn to be transparent to a degree, and at times vulnerable. You are giving others permission to peep into your life as an open book. But that's ok! Flaws and all, not just your strengths but they will see often on occasion your weakness even in moments of frustration, the highs, and the lows of life.

When we see the things that our mentors face, we can learn from their successes and mistakes. They are a living example of what to do if we are ever in similar situations. I have seen leaders who stayed in prayer during the difficult times, and only a select few knew what they were enduring. On the other hand, I witnessed other ministers attack the people who attacked them. Some mentors value family, and others were extremely ambitious while neglecting their family in the process. I learn to appreciate my mentor's achievements and failures, so I can be the best that God is calling me to become.

I discovered some of my mentor's vulnerabilities, and I had to make sure that I was mature enough to handle them. I was blessed to see another side of my leader. They are flesh and have feelings. Often, we tend to put our leaders on pedestals, but they are human. When we examine the lives of our mentors, be prepared to answer the hard questions.

1. Will you be able to handle your leader when they aren't operating underneath the anointing?
2. What happens if they are facing challenging circumstances?
3. If they are attacked, what is my role as their mentee?
    a. Do I pray for them, or do I abandon them in the process?
    b. Do I lift my mentor's arms like Aaron and Hur?
    c. Do I stand with them in the valley places?
4. Can I keep my leader covered as personal details are revealed about their life, or will I tell others?

Paul was very open. In 2 Timothy 3:10-11, "Timothy, you know all about my teaching, my way of life, my purpose, faith, patience, love, endurance, persecution, and sufferings." But now Paul comes to the end of his journey and he reaches out to his son Timothy to tell him, "I fought a good fight and I finished my course. I kept the faith." Now Timothy was able to watch Paul not just start a race but finish the race. Every starter is not a strayer! People start jobs, marriages, and ministries then quit. But Paul was a finisher and he finished his course. You can finish yours also.

"Getting the most out of life isn't about how much you keep for yourself but how much you pour into others."

— David Stoddard

CHAPTER 20

TAKE A CHANCE ON ME

Often times, mentors find themselves not just reaching for the most talented, gifted, or popular people. Every now and again, we have to go out on a limb and possibly put our neck on the line for people that may not be a favorite to many others. But in your heart, you see the potential. For instance, Saul of Tarsus, who would later become Paul, wrote two-thirds of the New Testament.

It was all because a man named Barnabas spoke up for Saul. Now converted to Paul is now a follower of Christ after God rocked his world, knocked him off his beast, and had spoken to them. God spoke to him by the prophet Ananias, lay hands on him! Because he prays now. Barnabas said, "I believe in him and I am willing to put my name on the line for him. I will support him and stand by him." He is chosen by God but that intimidated Saul.

In the previous chapter, I talked about how Barnabas came alongside Paul to mentor him and he did, but please don't miss this part of their lives. Barnabas not only helped him, but he took a chance on him. Who do you know that is in your life today that not only mentored you but took a risk to do it? We as mentors should be seeking out children and young adults who can be potential candidates for training, and maybe those who have some characteristics of leadership but need further development.

Morris Cerullo, a general of the faith, grew up in an orphanage. He was rebellious and hurt because he felt that no one loved him. Morris had a difficult childhood. One day, he was suicidal because he reached a breaking point. Before Morris could jump off the ledge, God spoke to Him. He was a little boy, but hearing the voice of the Lord rejuvenated his spirit and caused him to seek God for answers. There was a teacher that worked in the orphanage and she risked everything to mentor Morris. She brought him various magazines on Pentecostalism and the Gifts of the Spirit. Eventually, she got caught and lost her job. Morris and his teacher kept in contact. Since she took a chance on him and won him to the Lord, Morris ended up preaching to nations.

It's amazing what a little push, little support, little encouragement can do. So, who have you noticed, that if only they had that little extra something, it would make them ten times better, stronger, wiser, and more valuable? Don't be afraid to take a chance! I've known ballplayers that have gotten into trouble, kicked off the team, but picked up by another team. I've known high school dropouts who left school early but were encouraged by a mentor to go back to school and finish up, and many ended up going back and even going into the Army just because someone didn't give up on them. I can't begin to tell you all the positive words that have been spoken over my life by people who believed in me. I am that I am by the grace of God and all the great people he put in my life.

"I once looked at the world from only one view, but then one day, my view changed. Now, it's not about what I do see in my present, but it's about what I don't see that holds my future."

—Amber M. Brown

CHAPTER 21

JOIN ME AT THE TABLE

There are many mentees in the world needing mentors, but nobody invited them to the table. There are many different languages in the world, but none of them are without significance. 1 Corinthians 14:10 tells us that a voice, your voice, matters! It doesn't matter if you've always been left out or if you have always been chosen. You have a need to be at the table. We are told to speak up for those who may not be able to speak up for themselves, but to ensure progress and justice for those who have been crushed. In these last days, it is vital that we break the silence and ensure the need to feed!

When I say the need to feed, I am talking about mentorship in the sense of collaboration and dialogue being brought to a table where differences are present. Still, the similarity in vision teaches, builds, produces, and then gets passed on. This is when a connection takes place and a sense of purpose is created. We all have heard the saying "a closed mouth cannot get fed," and that is 100% true just as a closed ear will never know which way to take. You cannot feed the need of an individual if your voice is not heard.

God gave us our very own voice to create and to speak to the earth when it is in alignment with our assignment. Not only do our words create endless possibilities, but our words seal and stamp the approval of the mentorship relationship. After doing some research, I found out that in the womb, a baby at seven months that has a high heart rate is comforted by it's mother's voice and the heart rate slows down. You see, the sound of the mother's voice soothes the baby to the point of trust. This is the same case with a mentorship relationship. There must be a voice of wisdom given and there must be a willingness to be fed a different meal than they have ever had before in order to receive hope. Like a baby bird who awaits the mother to bring the food and to put in the baby bird's mouth, this is much like the need to feed in mentorship.

Think about a conversation over dinner. The family is gathered and eating a well-prepared meal, laughing, and enjoying conversation, that builds a relationship and that is what the world is lacking today is a relationship. More and more, the people are concerned about themselves and about how far to the top they can get all the while our country is in jeopardy and slowly fading away are the voices that are meant to change this world! A mentor understands the importance of just one person, one voice. It only takes one voice, sentence, or word to save someone's life. Just think about the impact that would be made if you had someone in your life that was constantly encouraging, correcting, preparing, and teaching you how to face the challenges in this lifetime so that you could very well help lessen the challenges for those who will eventually be the ones taking care of you. Don't you want people taking care of you who know what they are doing? That is what this world needs from you!

1. Would you say that you have become silent and have stepped back from sharing the very things that you have been taught?

2. Would you say that you have become silent in speaking up for yourself because you feel underestimated or that what you have to say doesn't matter?
3. Would you confess that there are visions, dreams, and goals that you have set for others but lack in setting for yourself because it is easier to push someone else than it is for you to take a risk?
4. What do you want to learn from your mentor and how can they help you?
5. What are your strengths and weaknesses?
6. How do you spend your time?
7. How do you handle conflict and correction?

These are important questions that you must ask yourself and are exactly the types of things your mentor needs to be bringing out of you. What better way than joining them at the table of mentorship.

"Being a good mentor is about asking questions. The more you can learn about your mentee and where she/he is in their career, the more you can offer. It's a two-way street, a two-way exchange of information and ideas and to be honest, I expect to get as much out of the mentorship as my mentee."

— Stephen Knight

CHAPTER 22

CAN YOU TRUST THE PROCESS?

Trusting the process means having faith that everything is unfolding as it should, even if you cannot see it happening. In the words of Mandy Hale, "What we are waiting for is not as important as what happens to us while we are waiting." Trust the process when you master it. Most of us only focus on the end-game or end goal. If that's the case, you're going to miss all the wonderful lessons and experiences along the way. The process is not a sprint; it is a marathon. It's not a microwave; it's a slow cooking crockpot.

The first step in trusting the process is having the faith to stay the course and the faith to wait. It's like taking a long drive by car, bus, train, or plane, but at the same time, you keep reminding yourself of the loveliest destination that awaits you there. In other words, it will be worth the wait if you endure the process of waiting.

There are so many examples I can use on this subject. I remember coming home from Texas with a severe toothache. I called my dentist because I needed relief. He said to me, "Ron, you need a root canal." After taking an x-ray, it was discovered that the tooth that was causing so much pain was very infected, so he explained to me the steps he would take to give me relief. Although relief was coming, I had to trust the dentist. Now, I must confess that the process was a bit painful, but it was worth it. The end result was relief!

However, when it comes to actual life, things take a totally different twist, it can actually have several meanings. For instance, let's look at the athlete trusting the process of their trainer. The trainer tries to get them into shape by preparing hard strenuous workouts from barbells to treadmills, weightlifting to bench pressing, push-ups to sit-ups, and then chin-ups. These exercises are all a part of the process, but if you stay in the gym, it will pay off.

Another example is a student trusting the process. They must choose which school to attend. Whether which institution they apply to depends on several factors, such as their GPA, extracurricular activities, recommendations, location, national board tests, college entry exams, programs, scholarship, loans, and grants. The student must trust that they have all the qualifications that school is looking for in the incoming freshman class. They must be confident and not get distracted by the competitiveness of the enrollment process. Once the students receive their acceptance letter, then they have to trust the process of getting all their materials and make sure tuition is paid. The right curriculum must be chosen for their desired career path. It's required to study for long hours to prepare for tests and finals. After a couple of years, the student will have a hard-earned degree.

Let's consider a building contractor. Now, trusting the process will be totally different than for an athlete or a student. It would require faith and patience. After looking at empty space or a piece of land, you understand the process that, in a few days, there will be a beautiful home or business on that property. Working toward a goal can be as exciting as the completion thereof. In the society in which we live, we never preach process. We embrace the promise and the promotion, but we sometimes hate the process.

So, while we are trusting the process, let's understand that it's okay to enjoy the journey along the way! Celebrate in stages, and don't be caught up in the end of a thing but understand that it's a step by step process, and that's okay, even if it is a long time.

> **"The key to success is being in the right place at the right time, recognizing that you are there, and taking action."**
>
> — Ray Kroc

CHAPTER 23

RIGHT PLACE RIGHT TIME

Best-selling novels are made up of mostly drama, power, and romance. This story is far from a piece of fiction. This is a true story written centuries ago, it's more than entertaining reading. It's a story of profound interplay of God's sovereignty and human will. We see in this story where God chose the place and opportunity and His people, Esther and Mordecai, who are really the main focal point in this text.

This book begins with Queen Vashti refusing to obey an order of the King Xerxes, her husband, and as a result, she was banished as the queen. This is what started the search for a new queen. King Xerxes sent out a decree to gather all the young beautiful Jewish women in the empire and bring them into the Royal Harem, and Esther was one of the chosen ones.

You can trust your mentor because they are God's appointed spokesperson in your life. We have to trust the God in them and realize that we need the wisdom they can impart so we can be successful. The right leaders want us to be successful as much as we do. For instance, Mordecai was Esther's biggest cheerleader. He believed in her and saw something in Esther that she couldn't see. He always placed other's needs before his own such as raising Esther when she was an orphan. Mordecai pushed her forward, checked on her, and watched over her progress (Esther 2:11). The right mentor will help you align with the will of God for your life.

Meanwhile, Mordecai became a government official, but he was also Esther's cousin. Now, there are many pieces of this story I could choose from to encourage you, but I want to focus on the fact that Esther was chosen but directed and mentored by her cousin, who gave her helpful advice. Always count it a blessing when God places the right people in your path. So, Mordecai advised Esther even after she was drafted and chosen to be queen. Mordecai's humility and loyalty to King Xerxes help set Esther in a state of favor with the King. The right mentor will cause favor and divine opportunities to come into your life as you submit to their godly counsel.

One day he contacted Esther and told her one of the reasons that she was chosen to be queen was so that she could, "Save the Jewish people." He made her realize that she was beautiful, but this was not just about her beauty. This was about DESTINY! Mordecai gave Esther hope and reminded her of her destiny. "Yet who knows whether you have come to the kingdom for such a time as this (Esther 4:14)?"

God placed him by her side to lead, guide, instruct, and mentor. He told her not to reveal her nationality at that moment, but he taught her the importance of timing. It is possible to say the right thing at the wrong time. He told her to wait on the opportune time to speak to King Xerxes, and she obeyed his instructions. When the time was right, she then revealed to King Xerxes Hamon's plot to kill the Jews, and because of Esther listening to her mentor, not only was her life saved, but her entire nation was saved! One thing that Esther learned from being mentored by Mordecai is to be bold. She watched Mordecai stand strong in his faith, being proud of his Jewish heritage, and not bow down to the wicked Haman (Esther 3:2-3).

She combined courage with careful planning. She was open to advice and willing to act on it, but I must insert here that it's not enough to receive advice, but we must act on it! It is also important to note that Queen Esther's actions were driven completely by her love and respect for her cousin as well as her love for her people, but because she listened even when it was risky, the outcome was great. It could have gone another way, but it didn't. You must trust your mentor even when it's difficult.

ABOUT THE AUTHORS

Amber M. Brown is a Spiritual Motivator and an Evangelist out of Poplar Bluff, Missouri. Amber's ministry, "Rise to the Mission", was birthed in 2017 after writing her first book, "Rise to the Mission." Her book is centered around deliverance, recovery, and restoration to build a foundation with a central focus on Jesus Christ. Amber travels all over the world as a sought-after motivational speaker and revivalist. She speaks on recovery, mental health, self-care, wellness, and restoration. Amber challenges us all to rise up, to stand in the truth and live every day in faith, allowing us to develop fully into the purpose for which God has designed us, regardless of our past or present circumstances. Her ministry begins in the home, as she is the mother of two wonderful blended children, Aiden and Kyleigh!

Amber is a Certified Peer Specialist with certificates in Wellness and Recovery and Mental Health First Aid. She is extensively involved in public relations and community networking in the mental health field. Amber is also an active member in her community's Crisis Intervention, Suicide Prevention teams, and the Community Advisory Board. Amber works full time with a local non-profit Certified Community Behavioral Health Organization, assisting and serving individuals in the community and surrounding counties.

Amber actively serves as a teacher at Probation and Parole, teaching "Recovery 2 Life" classes. These classes build and support individuals who are ready to transition from their past into a better and new future. She is an active member of Mt. Calvary Powerhouse Church in Poplar Bluff, MO, where she serves as a Sunday School teacher in the children's ministry as well as the church, under the guidance and leadership of Bishop

Ron Webb and First Lady Dr. Georgia Webb. Amber is an advocate for victims of domestic violence/abuse, drug addiction, suicide prevention/intervention, and pro-life foundations.

In her everyday walk, Amber keeps her focus on God and His plan. She uses her faith to assist in her focus on wellness and recovery, whether it's physical, mental, or behavioral health recovery. Amber uses all these traits to be a servant and speak at seminars, conferences, youth groups, schools, revivals, and recovery groups all over the United States and soon to be internationally. She speaks to individuals of all ages on how to apply their faith to the realities of life. She encourages individuals by sharing her story of overcoming sin and difficulty by the power of her maturing relationship with God, to rise up and reach their full potential in all areas of their lives.

Amber enjoys being outdoors and spending time with her family. She loves to participate in community events to help build unity within the community. She believes that in order to reach the world effectively, you must start in your own community first! Amber is consistently continuing her education and schooling in order to continue her growth as an individual and a daughter of Christ. She is currently a student at the International College of Bible Theology/School of the Prophets, where she is enrolled in classes to get her degrees in Theology and Counseling. She looks forward to achieving and reaching her goal of a doctoral with hard work and dedication.

Amber believes in building up others and inspiring them to grasp their identities within their community, while encouraging them to live their life abundantly in His power and grace. On this foundation of belief, two years ago, Amber started her "Rise to the Mission" interview shows. These shows focus on learning the missions of individuals and allowing them to share their stories on how they overcame adversity, trials, and tribulations. These individuals share the steps they took to "Rise to the

Mission" and provide resources and encouragement to others. If you would like to contact Amber for speaking engagements or book orders, email her at risetothemission@gmail.com.

ABOUT THE AUTHORS

Dr. Ron Webb is the pastor of Mt. Calvary Powerhouse Church in Poplar Bluff, Missouri. Pastor Webb has been in the ministry for over 35 years. He attended Three Rivers Community College in Poplar Bluff, Missouri. He majored in Business Administration and was a former "Raider" basketball player. He earned a Bachelor of Theology from the International College of Bible Theology, and a Master's of Pastoral Studies and a Doctorate of Theology from Midwest Theological Seminary.

The unique ministry of Dr. Ron Webb is evident as he is anointed in the area's leadership and church government. Dr. Webb has been considered by many to be "A Pastor to Pastors". His ministry is centered around "Restoration" and "Racial Reconciliation" and a sincere belief that we must "Reach the Lost at Any Cost". His preaching and teaching focuses on empowerment and hope. He often says that the church is where you go, but ministry is what you do outside the walls of the church. He believes that with God all things are possible! Dr. Webb has always had a heart for the lost "Give me the heathen for my inheritance". Many outreach ministries have been birthed to address the unmet needs of the church and the local community.

Dr. Webb is the C.E.O. and President of the S.E.M.O. Christian Restoration Center, a center for individuals who might need a second chance in life. He is the founder and a lead instructor of "School of the Prophets Bible College" in Poplar Bluff, Missouri. He is also the founder of the Heartland Family Center, an emergency shelter for families, an outreach ministry that was founded in 2007. The Heartland Family Center is owned and operated by Mt. Calvary Powerhouse Church.

Covenant Ministries is another ministry that was designed by Dr. Webb to advance God's Kingdom by providing a fellowship in which men and women of God find mutual encouragement, edification, counsel, and participate in leadership and ministerial training. Dr. Webb serves as the Bishop of Covenant Ministries.

He is a sought-after speaker, who has ministered the gospel of Christ both national and internationally, including Canada, Haiti, Russia, Jamaica, and England. Dr. Webb is active in the community and has served on both local and state-level boards.

Dr. Webb is an accomplished writer who has authored several books on leadership and racial reconciliation, including "Leadership from Behind the Scenes" and its companion workbook. This book focuses on challenges of Leadership, a must read for anyone in a leadership role. "Destroying the Roots of Racism", where he invites us to be a part of the solution and urges those hurt by racism not to let the adversity destroy their character, but instead let it define their character. "Exposing the Enemy from Behind the Scenes" (a sequel to Leadership from Behind the Scenes) to equip both established and emerging leaders to recognize the spirits that have infiltrated the church and stunted kingdom advancement. His latest book "Leadership Lessons: Things I Wish They'd Told Me" a minister's manual full of information and examples that will help new leaders to navigate challenges and move forward into their ministry.

Dr. Webb is married to Georgia Webb and they have 3 children: Ronnie Webb Jr., Tony Webb and Jackie (Webb) Brown all of Poplar Bluff, Missouri, and 4 grandchildren: Jerrell Brown, Jr., Jaxson Brown, Tony Webb and Maleah Webb. In his leisure time, Dr. Webb enjoys fishing and playing sports.

INDEX

A

abandonment, 18
accountability, 32–33, 53
adultery, 62
adversity, 110
affirmation, 19–20
ambitions, 42, 48
angels, 74, 76
anointing, 10, 34, 48, 50, 59, 89
Apostle Paul, 18, 57, 62
attention, 29, 34, 37, 44, 47, 76
authority, 74

B

balances, 53, 57
Barnabas, 1, 33, 92
battlefield, 33, 35–36
behavior, 1, 27–28, 61
belief, 107
blessing, 9, 54, 104
bookshelf, 70–71

C

careers, 49–50, 98

character, 19, 23, 75, 110
cheerleader, 103
children, 2, 6, 13, 28, 32, 35, 45–46, 59, 63, 65, 92, 110
Christians, 44, 63
classroom, 29, 34–35, 38
Coach Bess, 25–26, 28
coaching, 1, 25–27, 30
commandments, 2, 63
commitment, 22, 38
community, 63, 106–7, 110
compassion, 62, 67
confess, 18, 97, 100
consistency, 75
content, 49, 75
contrite spirit, 55
couple, 5, 32, 53, 100
court, 25–26, 28–29, 38
crops, 44

D

danger, 2, 22–23
death, 12
deliverance, 106
destination, 81
destiny, 24, 42, 104
discernment, 38
disciples, 1, 11, 61, 63
discipleship, 2, 63
disconnection, 19
dishonesty, 5
disputes, 65–66
distractions, 54, 78–81

division, 19, 75
dream, 11–12, 97

E

empowerment, 109
encouragement, 33, 54, 82, 108
endorsement, 41
evangelists, 58, 106
everlasting, 45

F

failures, 4, 28, 38, 83, 89
faith, 57–58, 62–63, 88–90, 93, 99–100, 105–7
faithfulness, 45
family mentorship, 2
fathers of faith, 57–58
faults, 38, 54
fish, 64
followers, 61, 92
foundation, 9, 41, 44–46, 57, 106–7
freedom, 19, 38
fruit, 16, 41, 46
fruitfulness, 11

G

gifts, 10, 16, 20, 23, 26–27, 59, 73, 76, 93
goals, 9, 29, 46, 49–50, 70, 79–81, 97, 99, 101, 107
government, 11, 104
grace, 93, 107
growth, 22, 28, 44, 70, 74, 78, 83, 107

guidance, 2, 6, 27, 36–37, 49, 59, 80, 82–83, 106
guide, 51, 53, 58, 69, 71, 86, 104

H

heart rate, 96
history, 5, 67, 71
holy life, 55, 62
Holy Spirit, 62–63
honor, 57
humility, 16, 49
hurt, 11, 23, 58, 84, 93, 110

I

impart, 43, 83, 103
individuals, 48, 58, 106–7, 109
inheritance, 45–46, 109
institution, 100
instructions, 62, 66, 104
instructors, 18, 57, 109
Intimidation, 10

J

jealous, 58, 75
Jethro, 1, 65–67
Jethro Principle, 65
Jezebel, 11
Jude, 74

K

karate, 15
kingdom, 49, 61, 104, 110
knowledge, 5, 45, 48, 50–52, 61, 69

L

leaders, 2, 7, 12, 22–23, 48, 53, 57–58, 72, 74–75, 84, 89, 110
leadership, 8, 10–11, 16, 23, 26, 48, 55, 66, 79, 93, 106, 110
leader's time, 50
legacy, 12–13, 44–46, 71
lessons, 15, 83, 99
life, 11–13, 26–29, 32–34, 45–46, 57–58, 60, 70, 73, 78–80, 88–89, 91–93, 96, 103–4, 106–7, 109
lifetime, 64, 70, 96
listening skills, 83
loyalty, 22, 104

M

mantle, 34
marathon, 21, 99
marketplace, 33
marriages, 5, 19, 53, 75, 90
mentality, 17
mentees, 1–2, 6–7, 11, 19, 25–28, 33–38, 41, 48–49, 54, 61–62, 74–76, 79, 82, 95, 98
mentoring, 1, 8, 19, 25, 27, 29, 34–35, 45, 48, 52, 62–63, 68, 70–71, 75, 88
mentors, 1–2, 6–7, 15–16, 18–19, 25–30, 33–39, 48–55, 61–63, 69–71, 74–77, 79–80, 82–83, 92–93, 95–97, 103–5
mentorship, 2, 9, 11, 13, 23, 25–27, 29, 33–37, 39, 53, 62, 69, 73–75, 78–80, 95–98

mentor's life, 50
mentor's vision, 10
mess, 75, 78, 80
military, 33–38
mindset, 78–79
ministry, 6, 10, 18–19, 23, 41, 49, 53–54, 58, 61, 66, 90, 106, 109–10
model, 62
money, 46, 58
Mordecai, 103–4

N

nationality, 104

O

obedience, 16, 76
opportunist, 11
orphan, 18, 104
orphanage, 93
orphan spirit, 17–19

P

partnership, 39, 48
passionate, 35, 67, 70
pastors, 58, 109
patience, 49, 89, 100
permission, 55, 75, 88
persecution, 89
perseverance, 47
players, 25–30

position, 6, 9, 29, 45, 74–75, 78
power, 9, 13, 74, 84, 103, 107
prayer, 61, 89
preachers, 19, 41
pride, 19, 23, 29, 74
process, 9, 32, 48, 54, 58, 69, 79, 89, 99–101
promises, 50, 79, 101
property, 10, 101
prophets, 23, 58, 107
punishments, 58

R

racism, 110
ranks, 37
recovery, 106–7
relationship, 1, 6–7, 9, 17, 19, 23, 35, 38, 45, 48, 59, 75–76, 96
relief, 84, 99–100
responsibility, 13, 25
restoration, 106, 109
revelation, 58, 69, 83
roles, 35–36, 48, 53, 76, 89
roots, 44, 46

S

sacrifice, 59, 65, 70–71
safety program, 23
servants, 61, 83, 107
sins, 23, 54, 61, 107
skills, 11, 16
society, 32, 36, 88, 101

soldier, 32–38
soul, 2, 11, 63
sovereignty, 103
spiritual father, 18, 58–59
steadfastness, 22
strength, 2, 4, 32, 63, 67, 88, 97
success, 4, 9, 11–12, 27–29, 32–33, 36–37, 41, 51, 89, 102
support, 1, 41, 49, 92
symbols, 2, 63

T

teachers, 1, 18, 27, 34–36, 39, 58, 63, 93, 106
trainer, 15–16, 34, 78, 100
training, 15, 23, 25, 32–33, 37, 39, 49, 58–59, 76, 93
transition, 9, 106
tribulations, 107
trust, 16, 18, 38, 67, 79, 85, 96, 99–100, 103, 105
truth, 19, 23, 41, 46, 58, 106

V

vessels, 13
victory, 12, 45, 80, 82
vision, 6, 12–13, 46, 50, 75, 95, 97
voice, 23, 55, 66, 82, 86, 93, 95–96

W

walls, 11, 46, 109
warfare, 48, 59
wisdom, 1–2, 4–7, 9–11, 25, 27, 29, 32–34, 44–47, 53, 55, 57, 66–67, 69, 71, 83–86

Y

yoke, 85
youth, 4, 10, 26, 88

DR. RON WEBB

www.ingramcontent.com/pod-product-compliance
Lightning Source LLC
Chambersburg PA
CBHW072036110526
44592CB00012B/1445